BOUNTY HUNTER

BOB BURTON

FOREWORD BY
RALPH "PAPA" THORSON

PALADIN PRESS
BOULDER, COLORADO

The Bounty Hunter
by Bob Burton
Copyright © 1984 by Bob Burton

ISBN 0-87364-296-1
Printed in the United States of America

Published by Paladin Press, a division of
Paladin Enterprises, Inc., P.O. Box 1307,
Boulder, Colorado 80306, USA.
(303) 443-7250

Direct inquiries and/or orders to the above address.

BOUNTY HUNTER

TRACKER INTERNATIONAL
175 Lakeside Boulevard
Suite 15 - 323
Landing, NJ 07850

The following quote has been used many times by other courts in reference to bounty hunting. The bounty hunter or surety . . .

". . . whenever they choose to do so may seize him and deliver him up to their discharge; and if this cannot be done at once they may imprison him until it can be done.
They may pursue him to another state; may arrest him on the Sabbath, and, if necessary, may break and enter his house for that purpose. The seizure is not made by virtue of new process. None is needed. It is likened to the rearrest by the sheriff of an escaping prisoner."

United States Supreme Court: *Taylor* v. *Taintor* 16 Wall, 36.

WARNING

BOUNTY HUNTING IS A DIRTY, DANgerous, and highly skilled occupation. This book is not meant to be an answer to the many problems, questions, and issues of this business.

The purpose of this book is to give an overview of the bountyman's pursuit of the criminals and fugitives the law allows him to pursue and arrest.

Without compliance with the various bail arrest laws of each state, the bountyman can be held as a common kidnapper. Read this carefully, then find a friendly bondsman, bountyman or attorney for some guidance.

Robert Burton
Santa Barbara, California

Contents

Acknowledgments

IN THE COURSE OF PUTTING THIS book together, I tapped some very creative people and took, on some cases, goodly amounts of their time. My first thanks goes to the legendary Ralph "Papa" Thorson. He and his lady, Wanda, shared their home and thoughts with me freely and often. Ralph's view of the bail business is honed by over nine thousand arrests and close to forty years as a bounty hunter.

Jim McConnaha, of Allied Fidelity, was extremely helpful in pinpointing some areas I had overlooked. His sharing of various publications and data was invaluable. Rex Palmer, Allied Fidelity attorney who passed away while this book was being written, detailed some of the vagaries of bail arrest procedure in various states. Gerald Franklin of the Santa Barbara, California, District Attorney's Office patiently explained some of the differences between Common Law and Statute. William Sandbach, writer and public relations advisor for the California Advisory Board of Surety Agents, responded willingly and quickly to my request for details on the bail bond situation in California.

And thanks to the following individuals who clarified points regarding bail arrest in their respective states:

x   **Acknowledgments**

Marilyn A. Ray, Administrative Aide to the Attorney General of Maryland and Kathryn Rowe, Staff Attorney; Phillip Lemman, Public Affairs Assistant, Department of Justice, State of Oregon; Ngoc T. Luong, Library Reference Assistant, Office of Pennsylvania Attorney General; and to the office of Ken Eikenberry, Attorney General of the State of Washington.

Yet the bottom line for errors, misjudgments, and misstatements are solely mine. I willingly, if not graciously, accept any wrath which might be directed at the book and its concepts.

Foreword

by Ralph "Papa" Thorson

EVEN A CASUAL OBSERVER WILL have to come to the conclusion that America's judicial system is in big trouble. Justice moves not only slowly but by many people's standards not at all. Guilty parties not only are not brought to trial, they are not even pursued when they fail to appear for their hearing or skip bail.

A morass of horseshit favors the criminal and places a burden on the victim. Vastly different penalties are assessed for the same crime by judges only a county or state apart. The real victims of our system are the actual victims themselves, witnesses, juries, and police officers. The ultimate penalty is paid by society; long and unreasonable delays in the system lead to justice delayed and eventually to justice denied.

Since the days of Pythias, men have pledged their word, honor, and goods to guarantee the appearance of their charges in court to answer the claims made against them. That concept eventually evolved into the American bail-bond system. Yet oftentimes bail-released criminals simply do not appear for their court appearance.

These bail fugitives flee to other states or localities. District attorneys refuse to extradite for reasons of cost and crowded court calendars. If it weren't for the bondsman and his bounty hunter, many of these fleeing fugitives would still be free today to ply their criminal activities.

The role of the bounty hunter is not diminished by modern attempts at bail reform. On the contrary, most attempts at bail reform have caused a massive increase in bail skips as evidenced by the recent studies of the Los Angeles and San Francisco experiments. Criminals abuse and use any attempt at bail reform for their own purpose, and this is no secret to anybody concerned with this problem.

The modern bounty hunter is ideally part attorney, part scientist, part psychologist, and part police officer. He is versed in languages of the ethnic groups in his area, strong and untiring, honest and sober. His appearance and demeanor are above reproach.

Sound impossible? Maybe.

But reality allows for the fact that any bounty hunter who takes his profession and trade seriously can study the professions listed above and realize that the skills involved in bounty work touch a bit of all of these.

The modern bounty hunter, once he has been tempered by several cases, realizes how little he knows and how much effort he must put into studying to acquire information and skills and seeking wise council. The bounty hunter also finds his skills being sought after for stolen-child recovery and skip tracing. These areas offer unlimited advancement for the bounty hunter willing to do his homework.

With the assignment of his first case by the bondsman, the bounty hunter opens up a great career. With a

The legendary Ralph "Papa" Thorson. With over 10,000 arrests to
his credit, Thorson is considered the "supreme" bounty hunter. Here
he holds his back-up gun, a S&W model .38 Bodyguard revolver and a
High Standard 12 gauge riot gun.

willingness to understand the problems facing bondsman and law enforcement officers, the bounty hunter realizes a more than equitable return for his own investment of time and effort.

Ralph "Papa" Thorson
North Hollywood, California

Preface

TO THE READERS OF THIS BOOK, I suggest caution. This book is intended to give an overview of the bail-arrest profession and the specific views of certain professionals. For the individual with academic interest in the bail-arrest procedure and its history, this book should serve its purpose.

For the individual who is interested in becoming a bounty hunter, this book provides a framework of information from which to work. For the imaginative reader, it allows a certain amount of vicarious participation. Any individual seriously interested in becoming a professional bounty hunter must weigh all the factors I have included in this book.

For example, do you have the necessary skills? Are you capable of learning those you lack? Have you considered the possibility of being seriously hurt? Do you have the capability of dealing with members of all strata of society in a positive way? All these factors must seriously be taken into consideration before you expose yourself to injury and possible ridicule (even a lawsuit) by offering yourself as a bounty hunter to a legitimate bondsman, then failing miserably.

As a bounty hunter, you operate as a paralaw-enforcement agent; you bear all the risks attendant to the badge yet have none of its covering factors such as liability insurance, health insurance and psychological power. If you succeed in overcoming your initial problems and self-doubts and if your recovery ratio escalates, you may find yourself in a valuable and rewarding profession.

But don't ever expect to be nominated head of the Chamber of Commerce of your city. The word "bounty hunter" is laden with colorful and dubious associations. Hell, even your mom will wonder.

If you have the moxie and muscle, try to make a connection with a local bounty hunter. Ask your local bondsman (or bondswoman) who he would use for a jumper. Anticipate the fear and the "Pucker Factor" you will experience on your first encounter. What if your first case is the local biker chieftain who jumped bail on a drug-torture rap?

I suggest you find a buddy as big or bigger than yourself who is willing to go along on a pickup. Educate yourself with all the reading and studying you can do on police science. But remember as you turn each and every page in this book, field experience is the only teacher that gives a diploma—in the form of a healthy check naming you as the payee. If you "make your bones" and survive, you will find yourself in a most unique profession with the most unusual members of society.

Best of luck and stay off the skyline.

Robert Burton
Santa Barbara, California

1. Hunters Defined

FEW OCCUPATIONS IN THE TWENtieth century have remained as unchanged as bounty hunting has. Today, the bounty hunter, or bountyman, is that individual who pursues and arrests the bail bond jumper. Working as the appointed agent of the bondsman who posted bail, the bounty hunter has the legal authority to pursue and arrest the defendant who skipped out. Yet, since he works as an independent contractor, the bounty hunter is not paid unless he finds and brings into custody the fugitive, hence the term "bounty."

In earlier times, the bounty hunter was the headhunter who sought fugitives listed on the "Wanted—Dead or Alive" posters that were posted by various government agencies. In the nineteenth century, undeveloped lands west of the Mississippi attracted men on the run. Long distances separated the rough, dusty, western towns, and police officers were in scarce supply. Bounty hunters seeking fugitives were tolerated, if not encouraged.

Various cattlemen's associations had their own police forces authorized to track down and bring to justice cattle and horse thieves. Even today, the Texas and Southwestern Cattle Raisers Association out of Fort Worth, Texas, has a very efficient deputized force of men who do nothing but pursue cattle thieves. In the past, bonding companies hired in-house detectives to find jumpers, and where the bondsman was liable, he hunted his own man.

With the turn of the century, however, and the diminution of the Wild West, a new form of bounty hunter emerged: the businessman's bounty hunter.

Anyone arrested in this country for the commission of a crime is entitled to bail except in cases of capital offense. All but the most heinous crimes allow for the defendant to be released on bail. In return for the bail bondsman posting the stipulated amount of bail, the person charged is released from jail. He is not "free"; the prisoner is in the custody of the bondsman. To secure the bail to the bondsman, the prisoner pays the bondsman a fee, usually 10 percent of the posted bail amount. For example, a crime such as rape may have the bail amount set at $50,000. In that case, the prisoner pays the bondsman 10 percent or $5,000.

Usually the bail is secured with property or real estate, often pledged by the prisoner's family or friends. Bail can be posted within hours of the individual's arrest or even days later, depending on the prisoner's ability to raise the money to buy the bail.

The purpose of bail is not to punish the prisoner, nor to enrich the coffers of the state, nor to provide an occupation for the bondsman; bail helps to ensure the appearance of the defendant at his hearing, while permitting him to lead the semblance of a normal life.

Later, if the defendant does not show up in court, the judge issues a bench warrant for his arrest. At this point the bondsman gets pissed off. The person he has posted bail for—let's say it was $10,000—has defaulted on his promise to appear and the bail has been forfeited. The bondsman's money is now in jeopardy.

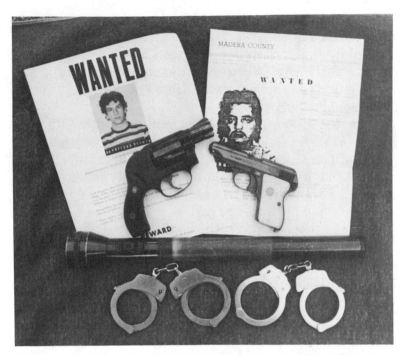

A bounty hunter needs a good description of the fugitive he's seeking, flashlights, handcuffs, and weapons for self-defense. He also needs intelligence and maturity to know when to use them.

At first, the bondsman hopes the police will rearrest his man before the time rolls around when he must pay the forfeited bail. That time varies from state to state and is from ten days to one year. In California, it is six months. If, in California, on the 181st day (six months), the defendant has not been found, the bondsman must fork over the $10,000 (or whatever amount) to the county or state governmental entity that required the posting.

The bondsman is now out $10,000.

But let's go back. Right after the defendant has posted bail—and before he has to appear in court (usually ten to thirty days)—the bondsman simply keeps track of his schedule on a calendar listing his bailees. He may be posting bail for three to ten or more cases a day, depending on the size of the city. When his bailee doesn't show for his hearing is when the bondsman first knows there's going to be trouble.

For the first three or four months on the smaller bonds ($10,000 or less), the bondsman hopes that the police will make a routine traffic stop on his man, run his name through the big computer in the sky, and, finding that he's a wanted man, rearrest him. This will save the bail bondsman his forfeited bail.

After a time, however, the bondsman starts to worry. After all, he reasons, the police are more or less looking for hundreds of fugitives. With $10,000 on the line, he starts to sweat. That's when he calls on a specialist. That's when he picks up the telephone and dials the number of a trusted bounty hunter.

2. Whose Authority?

THE AUTHORITY THAT A BOUNTY-man operates under derives from Article 4, section 2 of the U.S. Constitution and the Act of February 12, 1793, which was passed to give effect to it. It reads in part:

> A person charged in any State with treason, felony or crime, who shall flee from justice and be found in another state, shall, on demand of the executive authority of the State from which he fled, be delivered up to be removed to the State having jurisdiction of the crime.

Laws have been passed in all states (which can be found in the Penal Codes) allowing the bondsman, referred to as the *surety,* to pursue and arrest his man, the *principal,* in any state in the country. This authority may be extended to his *agent.* That is, the bondsman may appoint someone to pursue and arrest his fleeing principal.

A court decision upholding this concept held:

> I see nothing, on general principles, against allowing this power to be exercised by an agent

or deputy; and no case is found where the right
has been denied.

The decision also stated:

> . . . the law recognizes the act of an authorized
> agent as equal to that of the principal (the
> bondsman). . . . *Nicholls* v. *Ingersoll,* 7 Johns, 154

The bondsman and the bounty hunter are not required to have a warrant or order of the court. The
authority of the bail bondsman to arrest the fleeing subject has been compared with that of a police officer re-
arresting an escaping prisoner. No new process of law is
necessary.

In most areas of the country, California for one, the
bounty hunter must have a certified copy of the bail
agreement when delivering the prisoner to jail. This is
especially necessary when the bondsman arrests the subject *before* he jumps bail. Suppose the bondsman gets information that his man is intending to flee the country
before his court appearance date. With his man in
Bermuda or Costa Rica, his chances of a pickup diminish
greatly. The bondsman may then have his man picked up
even if the reasons are no more than suspicion.

In this situation, the certified copy is very necessary.
Once the man has jumped bail, however, the fact that he
is a fugitive and has a warrant out on him due to his
failure to appear in court makes a citizen's arrest very
legal. Personally, I always request a certified copy, however, and you should have a certified copy in your hands
when surrendering the fugitive to a local jail.

Perhaps the most quoted law on the right of a bounty
hunter to arrest comes from the United States Supreme

Court. It comes from an 1872 decision involving a man who jumped bail in Connecticut and was rearrested by the bondsman (some bondsmen are also bounty hunters) and taken back for trial.

The defendant protested the right of rearrest and the issue went all the way to the U.S. Supreme Court. The court upheld the bondsman's right to pursue across state lines and arrest. The wording used by the Supreme Court has been upheld and states in part:

[The bondsman or bounty hunter] Whenever they choose to do so may seize him (the fugitive) and deliver him up in their discharge; and if this cannot be done at once they may imprison him until it can be done. They may pursue him to another state; may arrest him on the Sabbath, and, if necessary, may break and enter his house for that purpose. The seizure is not made by virtue of new process. None is needed. It is likened to the rearrest by the sheriff of an escaping prisoner. (US Supreme Court, *Taylor* v. *Taintor* 16 Wall, 366)

And that, essentially, is the law under which a bountyman operates. This law does not, however, extend to foreign countries. If a bountyman pursues his subject into another country, he has no legal mantle under which to hide. The subject has broken no law in his new country but the bounty hunter has—kidnapping. Two American bountymen are now undergoing a trial in Canada for entering that country and picking up a fugitive wanted in Florida. In the countries to the south, there is a little more leeway. I have picked up men in Mexico with nothing more than luck and some dollars to buy the goodwill of the local *policia.*

The right of a bail bondsman to rearrest through his agent, the bountyman, has been established by courts and law in the United States, yet much is misunderstood about the undertaking. Not only are most police officers still uncertain about how legal a bounty hunter is, so are the courts and district attorneys.

I have been stopped many times by a police officer who has seen me struggling with an arrested subject. When the cop sees two or three men wrestling with one man, his first thought is that he's happened upon a mugging. His response is to pull a firearm and aim it at the bounty hunters. Timing can be extremely important and quick identification is a must.

What I've written here is in no way the last word on the legality of bounty hunting. You need to be informed on the laws where you will be working *and* the customs of those states. Each state has a penal code section on the matter of bail arrests. It is your obligation to yourself to look in the penal codes for a list of the requirements and laws governing bail arrests. Never overlook going in to visit your local district attorney. One doesn't have to be a criminal to get an appointment with these public employees.

3. Virgin Territory

FEW BOUNTY HUNTERS STARTED out to become bounty hunters. Everyone I have known just sort of blundered into it. Some were asked by a friend to go along and help pick up someone who had jumped bail.

My first job was in Brooklyn, New York in 1961. All I had to do was sit in the car in the alley behind an apartment house and keep the motor running. The two guys I was working for met me in a bar on Flatbush Avenue through a mutual friend. To this day, I'm not sure if they were using me for a patsy or valued me as a trusted worker. I suspect with the passing years the latter. In any case, I made thirty-five dollars (when gasoline cost under a quarter a gallon) which I thought was big money—and it was easy money. The most startling point of it all was when they pushed, pulled and beat this huge Italian guy into the back seat. I wasn't at all prepared for that. They looked like they were in control, though, and all they said was "drive." We took him to the precinct in Brooklyn on Fourth Avenue, and my two bosses disappeared inside with him.

Months later I found out that he was part of one of the gangs of Mafiosi then warring in Brooklyn. The two guys that picked him up went to Florida for some R&R (and health) until things cooled down. Due to my relatively unknown status, no one ever questioned me. I've always wondered how close I came to floating in Sheepshead Bay.

Right after this incident I went back into the Marines and had to put my budding career in bounty hunting on the back burner.

There is, however, one requirement for being a hunter: one must be in good-to-excellent physical and mental condition. This is an absolute. One of the basics of this business is that you must be able to subdue a prisoner. And while it's smart to take along someone big for the pickup, the hunter still has to jump in and take the lead, possibly in hog-tying the subject.

Let's say you are interested in bounty hunting and approach a bondsman for a contract (more later on how to do this). The bondsman will look at you and immediately size you up. If he sees before him a 155-pound, twenty-three-year-old dude dressed in a black turtleneck, black watch cap, and black SWAT-team pants tucked into shiny, black boots (as one would-be hunter presented himself), all the hunter will get is a polite request to get the hell out of the office. Bounty hunting is more subtle than obvious, more finesse and muscle than assault and noise.

Essentially, there are two ways of getting into bounty hunting: 1. Assisting an experienced bounty hunter (best); and 2. Getting your first contract "cold" from a trusting bondsman (unlikely). If you want to pursue this, go around to some of the bail bondsmen in your area and introduce yourself. Ask them for the name and/or phone number of whomever they use for bounty hunting. Chances are they will be reluctant to do so. It's just part of the business. Suspicion is always there. Maybe you will be asked to leave your number and told that somebody will call you. Or approach a friendly cop for some suggestions.

The telephone is the "most dangerous weapon known to man" in the hands of an experienced skip tracer. Here bounty hunter Bob Burton makes contacts for leads on a fugitive's whereabouts.

Usually the warrants officer can help. He is the officer who is aware of all the fugitives outstanding from his area. Bounty hunters most often deal with warrants officers; at least that has been my experience.

Chances are that there are no bounty hunters in your area. I don't think there are over five to ten people in the country making a full-time living at it. Maybe another fifty to two hundred make a good part-time income at it, and who knows how many do it once or twice a year?

This can be good and bad for the beginner. Perhaps the bail bondsmen in your area are desperately looking for someone to help out. If you do present yourself cold in a bondsman's office, it would be wise to take a friend with you, someone who is also muscular and competent looking. Remember that the bondsman wants his people brought back for appearance in court, not beaten up. He will judge you on the way you look and what you say. Don't come across like some macho jerk. Remember that 80 percent of bounty hunting is detective work; you need to look and act like you have the intelligence and physical prowess to handle the *entire* job.

If you are lucky, the bondsman will have a small and not-too-risky case for you. Maybe someone has jumped bail on a child support case and the bail is $3,000. The usual fee for a bounty hunter is 20 percent of the bail, making the commission on this case $600. On the higher bails some negotiating is often the rule.

Anticipate splitting the fee with your partner if you work it equally. I prefer hiring someone to come along with me for the pickup. I do all the detective work and cover all the costs, and then usually I pay $150 to $200 a day to my helper. If I am working with a partner, it's a fifty-fifty split. Of course, if the contract is his, the situation might be turned around.

Otherwise, if you can make contact with a local bounty hunter, you might be able to sell him on why he should use you as an assistant. But why does he even talk to you? Maybe you are exceptionally big. Perhaps you have a driving personality, can speak Spanish, Italian, Hebrew or some other language that is helpful. Perhaps you have some money and are willing to buy your way into his business. Or perhaps, and most importantly, you are willing to assist him at no cost as a free apprentice.

If you really want to get some experience, working for nothing for a while may be the only way. Sort of a work-study program. Yet, I suspect that any bounty hunter worth his profession will pay you. A big plus for you would be an introduction by a mutual friend. Essentially, the bounty hunter wants to know that you won't cut and run at the first sign of trouble. He may start you off as a driver or maybe the third partner on what is a two-man team and pay you a few bucks.

Should a bounty hunter take you under his wing as an assistant, more of a gofer in reality, you should consider yourself lucky. But if you have a current job, for God's sake, don't quit it. There may be long spells between checks with your new employer.

But despite the legal legs they stand on and the monetary gain they may enjoy, bountymen are considered near-criminals by some police officers, bail bondsmen, citizens, and even other bountymen. And, there may be a bit of the truth in that view. In order to think like a criminal and blend in with the criminal element, a bountyman must possess some innate cunning and have developed some experience with and some knowledge of criminal activities.

In order to apprehend a criminal or fugitive fleeing from some legal or civil authority, the bountyman must think one foot ahead of him to anticipate his moves. To learn to do this, there is only one primary requisite: time. The bounty hunter needs time in the field and time in pursuit to gain experience. I can give you the benefit of my experiences in this book, but time is the mother and father of success.

Your ultimate success, however, depends on how smart you are, how cunning you are, and how physically strong you are. I offer no pretense about having all the answers and I'm not particularly big, yet my rate of success is roughly 67 to 70 percent—enough to be considered successful. When I worked for an insurance company, my success rate went up to 100 percent—almost. The reason was that they footed some up-front expense money, and I could hunt, bribe, and buy information with cash. Working for a bondsman cold and on "commission" means that the previous bounty has to fund the next project.

Remember, too, that if someone jumps bail, he not only angers the bondsman, he also betrays the person who signed as collateral on the bond. This is the person from whom the bondsman will try to recover his losses on the bail. This is the person who pledged his home, salary, car or whatever in order to get his friend, lover, or spouse out of jail.

If a bail is in the one-thousand-to-three-thousand-dollar range, don't be afraid to ask for 40, 50, or 80 percent of the bail, especially if the fugitive has fled out of state. Sometimes the collateral is strong, and the person who put up the security is willing to pay to have the fink he signed for brought back at any cost. If you can apprehend him, it's so much the better for you.

4. Trade Tools

BOUNTY HUNTING IS ESSENTIALLY mental work; it is closer to the occupation of a detective than that of a military man. The tracking, locating, and capture of a fugitive involves the use of certain specialized equipment that was unavailable to early-day bounty hunters. Modern-day bounty hunters spend most of their time working with one main piece of electronic equipment—the telephone, the most important device that the hunter utilizes. Ralph Thorson calls the telephone "the most dangerous weapon known to man." This taken-for-granted domestic appliance enables the hunter to reach out to contacts, snitches, and leads throughout the country with ease and relatively low cost.

Once he has found his man, however, the bounty hunter needs a number of specialized tools when he moves in for the pickup. These devices and weapons are used in surveillance, monitoring conversations, and, most importantly, self-defense.

However, let me give you a word of caution here: be careful how you use your equipment to physically influence others. Lawsuits eat up a lot of money, and if you really hurt someone—however unintentionally—you may find yourself the fugitive fleeing from some cunning bountyman. Here are a few facts that might help you remember to control your anger or panic.

"I'm gonna whump you up alongside the haid, boy," drawls a Southern do-gooder on the late night movie. People are always entertained when they see their TV hero get slammed up "alongside the haid" by a vertical buttstroked .45 and wake up groaning a few minutes later. However, hitting people on the head can get them *and you* into serious trouble.

The human head can only take so much pounding by metal or hard wooden objects. When you are arresting an unruly individual, you may feel the need to break something over his or her head. Don't do it! Serious injury could result. You may soon have a comatose individual on your hands, possibly with blood coming out of his nose and ears. On the other end of the scale, your blow to his head may do no more than enrage your man.

If serious injury results, the jumper (now considered the victim) or his family will sue you and the bondsman for excessive force. Even worse, he could be severely injured, suffer brain damage and require constant care for the rest of his life. Remember what can happen to a prize fighter getting hit on the jaw or cheekbone with a "soft" sixteen-ounce glove: a number of professional fighters have died in the last few years.

All the above warnings do not apply if you are trying to take in a fugitive who has a long history of violence and is resisting you to the point where your life may be in danger. There you have the right to use what may, at some other time, be unreasonable force.

Ralph Thorson uses a good analogy to explain this. "Suppose you have a yardstick. Let's say that the first twenty-six inches represent the point below which you hit a man and simply enrage him; you turn him into a bull of wild strength.

"Inches twenty-seven and twenty-eight represent the point where you hit him perfectly: no injuries, just a short duration of being stunned, or possibly unconscious, but with no aftereffects. It's just right.

"But inches twenty-nine on up to thirty-six represent the area of severe injury to the individual: blood clots, internal bleeding, fracture of the skull, all kinds of internal problems."

Ralph's point is well taken. Small chance exists for hitting with just the right force with the perfect (whatever that is) blunt instrument. If you must hit someone with something other than your hand, hit him on the elbows, wrists, knees and collar bone. I guarantee these points are painful.

Flashlight

This is not to be taken for granted. A good flashlight of extra strong frame will both be durable and serve as a club in a life-threatening situation. The blast a 35,000 candlepower light beam can produce on your brain is overwhelming. Flooding a room with this kind of light will blind, demoralize, and overwhelm a suspect or fugitive.

Several manufacturers produce flashlights with a capacity up to 135,000 candlepower. One manufacturer, Stream Light, produces a light up to 1,000,000 candlepower. It'll knock your socks off.

For bounty hunting, one needs a flashlight that is easily carried, strong enough to handle a tremendous amount of abuse, and heavy enough to whack a bad guy alongside the head in a serious situation. It should do all this and still give enough candlepower to both illuminate and blind your subject. Several manufacturers fill this

Good handcuffs such as these from Smith & Wesson and a high-beam flashlight are useful tools. The fugitive's hands are cuffed behind his back. A flashlight will disorient a person in a darkened room and can be used as a club in dire circumstances.

bill. They are: Stream Light, L.A. Screw Products (Police Equipment Division), Magna-Lite, and Tekna.

Stream Light produces an SL series of lights of 15,000, 20,000, and 35,000-candlepower. Coded the SL15, SL20, and SL35, they are exceptional quality lights. They are equipped with a quartz-halogen bulb and rechargeable nickel-cadmium batteries. The 35,000 candlepower light will knock your socks off. These lights are not cheap, being in the $100 to $175 range, but then again neither is your life and health.

L. A. Screw Products produce a fine system of lighting. While their flashlights do not give the same intense light as the Stream Light, the price range is perhaps more attractive. Their Code Four uses a regular D-cell battery with the conventional bulb. And like the Stream Light, the battery tube is made of no-slip knurled aluminum. They come in two- through seven-battery models and are priced in the $30 to $40 range.

Mag-Lite of Ontario, California, produces an excellent, solid, machined-aluminum light. It comes in various sizes up to a seven battery, is shatterproof, waterproof, and reasonably priced from $40 and lower. The beam is adjustable from spot to flood.

Tekna Products produces some fine designer-type lights as well as knives. While not of the battering-ram nature as the previously mentioned lights, they are more than sufficient for bounty work. One of these lights, the Tekna-Lite 8, uses eight AA alkaline batteries and a Krypton bulb to produce an incredible 18,000-candlepower beam ample enough to illuminate any darkened bedroom.

Weapons

The ugly reality of bounty hunting is that someone is going to shoot at you—or at least try to. You should have a handgun and have it available for easy use. This is not to say that you will approach every fugitive with it on your person. Yet as you develop a profile on your target, you will find some prove to be high-risk cases and warrant your carrying a piece with you.

Consider two things: concealability and stopping power. Nothing less than a .38 Special, with a 9mm or .45 recommended. The weapon should be dependable and big enough to stop someone in his tracks.

I will offer no suggestions as to a handgun here other than caliber. I suggest, however, that the gun you pick be of a major and well-known manufacturer who has plenty of years of experience in making combat-style handguns. I also suggest you put yourself through one of the finer schools in this country that will teach you reaction shooting.

You should also have a shotgun, preferably a 12-gauge, with a short stock. The Ithaca Bear Stopper, the

Mossberg M-500, and the Remington are good places to start.

A boot knife is also something that you might consider. In pursuing some fugitives, you will need all this stuff. Yet in the vast majority of the cases, you won't. Don't think you have to track your man like he was game and fully arm yourself. Your best weapon will be your brain. I don't want to leave you with the impression that you will be getting into a major gunfight every other weekend.

In all cases, you must also be aware of the various laws pertaining to carrying weapons in an urban area. See the chapter on concealed weapons.

Handcuffs

Here's a very necessary tool of the trade. Handcuffing your man with his hands behind his back and delivering him to the slammer is the last task you will perform with each individual fugitive.

Two brands of cuffs stand out: Peerless and Smith and Wesson. For many years S&W had the corner on cuffs with their Model 90. Recent changes and the introduction of the Model 100 and the Model 103 (the lightweight one) have resulted in a somewhat lesser product, in my opinion. The key jamming in the Model 100 and 103 is a complaint I've heard from law enforcement people I have spoken to.

Peerless makes an excellent nickel-plated cuff. I have not heard anything bad about the Peerless brand. Both the Peerless and S&W sell in the neighborhood of $20. Don't buy some cheap brand and have 250 pounds of irate jumper sitting behind you in your car break the cuffs and then decide your neck needs breaking. Have at least two pairs with you at all times.

Ralph Thorson prefers the Colt .45 Government Model as his personal handgun. His has an ambidextrous safety, Pachmayr grips, and stainless moving parts. The Brechia .22 LR boot gun (inset) is a back-up.

This S&W Model .38 Bodyguard revolver is a good-size handgun for most people. It is accurate and reliable.

Binoculars

This is a nice-to-have item. Binoculars enable you to monitor an individual whom you suspect is your man without him being easily able to spot you. Due to the improved, modern lens, your ability to see during the pre-dawn and late evening hours is enhanced.

Regardless of the manufacture, get binoculars with coated lenses, which even cheap binoculars have these days. Test the quality of coatings by holding the lenses at waist level and at such an angle to allow the overhead light to reflect on the lenses. You will see the coating. It should be even and bluish-purple to amber in color. This is the coating that reduces the incoming light.

Get some lightweight binoculars in 7, 8, or even 10 power with a lens diameter of 35 or 50. Higher lens diameters will give you a wider field of view which is unnecessary for watching a suspect.

If you can afford the extra cost, get binoculars with rubber coating or "rubber armor." This will give an extra dimension of protection for the battering binoculars take. And lastly, find a pair with a twilight factor of 15 or 17 to allow for the darker hours surveillance. Stick with brand names such as Bausch and Lomb, Bushnell, or Zeiss. At the risk of contradicting myself, one can find quality binocs in lesser known names. Whatever you do, don't get a pair so large you cannot conceal them easily should your man glance your way or so heavy that they are unwieldy or awkward to hold for any length of time.

Night Vision Devices

These are nice and expensive, a real luxury. Seek the passive design, as these are usually the lighter, in the two-pound range. The cost will be in the thousands, and the devices are illegal in New York and California. Both active and passive models can be tested and bought at most gun shows or well-equipped Army/Navy stores. Don't bother rushing out to buy any in the early stages of your bounty hunting career.

Portable Communications

Hand-held communications devices are another luxury item in this business but only for the beginning hunter. Keeping a suspect under surveillance until a pickup is enhanced with communication between the people involved in the surveillance.

Hand CB units are readily available to the bounty hunter with enough money. Don't waste your time on anything under $100. The 40-channel CB unit can be found in any Radio Shack or like store. They put out a five-watt power and have a range of several miles, more than enough to tail the average jumper. These are generally in the price range of $130 to $150.

A quantum leap has happened in the communications area in the last few years with the "tactical radios." These little honeys are the devices worn with a light headset and a receiver on the belt. These units allow the hands to be free which is ideal when holding a flashlight and weapon and approaching the suspect's door. They are powered by either 9-volt DC batteries or six AA penlight batteries. They come in either voice actuated (VOX) or push-to-speak mode. The latter seems more effective when stalking someone as the first part of a word is cut off in the former mode when it activates. The tactical radios are very cheap at $50 to $60 apiece. Using FM, as they do, eliminates most any chance of interference. When buying these, one must buy at least two at a time so the channels are the same. Range is limited (and so is interference) to within half a mile maximum; the average is one-quarter of a mile.

BB Gun

Do you need a BB gun? Yes. This obviously won't be a defensive weapon, but still it's nice to have. Suppose you want to get a little closer to a fugitive's house or apartment at night, but a strategically placed floodlight illuminates your path. That BB gun would come in mighty handy. It can also be used to drive away a particularly pesky guard dog. Even a couple of hits plinking against the bad guy's windows or door just might drive him outside wondering what those pesky kids were up to only to meet a couple hundred pounds of bounty hunter.

The main criteria are quiet discharge and reloading without too much noise. Nothing fancy, even a cheap pistol will do. Stay away from the .22- or .177 type of air gun. Remember, you don't want to destroy too much property or injure pets or humans.

Stun Gun

One tool some bounty hunters find quite valuable is the stun gun. It definitely has the power to stop—without permanently injuring—a very large hunk of beef. This handy item mechanically propels a bean-bag-type projectile filled with buckshot at a high rate of speed. Shot into a man's chest, it will knock him backward and incapacitate him for about as long as would a hardy punch. He'll only suffer a black-and-blue spot from the impact, and in the meantime, you can move in and handcuff him. The only trouble is that the stun gun is illegal in certain states, one of them being California.

The type of stun gun I'm familiar with is the Prowler-Fouler, which is made of high-impact plastic and costs

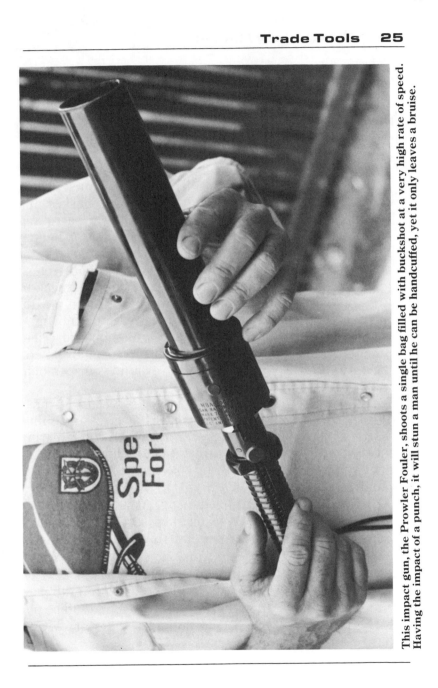

This impact gun, the Prowler Fouler, shoots a single bag filled with buckshot at a very high rate of speed. Having the impact of a punch, it will stun a man until he can be handcuffed, yet it only leaves a bruise.

$150 or so. In states where such a weapon is legal, you can depend on the impact to take down a hard-charging opponent. There's only one shot, however; once the bean bag has left the gun, it had better find its mark or you will have one hellishly mad guy coming your way.

Miscellaneous

A good-sized bag to put all this in is a must. Now, with your equipment in your satchel and you parked in a dark alley watching your man, chances are a patrolling cop will think you are a burglar and bust you for having "burglar's tools in your possession." So have plenty of documentation and the certified copies on or about you so you can identify yourself. This is why I usually check in with the watch commander if I am operating in an unknown area or, more realistically, where I'm unknown.

Some other things nice to have are: clipboards, pencils and pens, a karate-style groin protector, gloves, etc. The list is limitless and will develop around your personal style.

A little box to hold some other very necessary items is useful. Some of these items are: spare batteries and bulbs, a bottle of aspirin and Alka Selzer (for when you're eating fast-food while working), spare handcuffs and keys, extra paper and pencils and anything else you discover you need all of a sudden.

I haven't even mentioned a car. Assuming you have one, I hope it isn't a two-seater or a small sub-compact. Cramming a prisoner into one of these is like trying to shove a size eleven foot into a size nine shoe—not to mention very dangerous.

The ideal car is at least a mid-size car, preferably an American-made, with four doors. The prisoner will be put on the right hand side (never behind the driver) with a guard next to him.

5. Skip Tracing

SKIP TRACING IS THE VERY HEART and soul of bounty hunting. The fugitive cannot be arrested until you first find him. This skill is called *skip tracing,* which involves logic, deduction, imagination, deception, detective work, a bit of psychology, and lots of patience.

You are tracing a fugitive who has deliberately made himself unavailable. Most runaways, however, are not skilled at eliminating their trail. This paper trail, however minor, will ultimately lead you to their door.

It is surprising the number of fugitives who can be found at their addresses or jobs. The fact of the matter is that most bail skippers do not take their acts seriously. They feel that any time they desire, they can solve their problems by going back to court and settling up by paying a fine.

This, of course, excludes the man facing a hard term for a serious crime such as bank robbery, rape, or any violation that will land him in the slammer. He is more knowledgeable about the system. This person flees because he cannot cope with the court system, has no attorney he trusts, has overwhelming evidence against him, or has a reason that produces the "flight is right" mentality. He may flee as close as the rural home of a nearby friend or as far away as another state. Or he may stay within a block of his old home, perhaps with a new name and I.D. Your job is to find and arrest him.

After a man fails to show for his court appearance, he is considered to have "skipped bail." While this is a loose term, it generally is indicative of an individual who has no intention of standing trial for his charged crimes. Of course, it also leaves the bail bondsman out on a limb, as he is the one who bailed him out based on that promise to appear.

A judge then issues a bench warrant for the fugitive's arrest, and the police are notified. If the crime is a serious one against another person or involving valuable property, the police will devote a goodly amount of attention to the case. This also depends on the size of the town or city and the case load of the detectives. The bounty hunter has the advantage of being able to work the case day after day without bureaucratic distractions.

Generally, the detectives give some attention to the case as soon as it crosses their desks. Usually a visit to the last known address or place of employment will be made. If the fugitive was interested in surfing the day of the court appearance and was not actually fleeing prosecution, he will be found. This surprised individual will be handcuffed and led away a much wiser person.

But the fugitive who is serious about his intent in not appearing in court will have taken steps to avoid detection. Friends willing to lie will state that he is in Florida for the rest of the year or working an oil field in Mexico. He will have changed jobs as it is harder to get a boss or personnel officer to lie.

You may step into the case several months after the man has jumped. Some bondsmen wait this long hoping that the police will pick up the man, which eliminates the need to pay the bounty hunter his fee. Unfortunately, it also means the fugitive is on guard and that the trail is months old.

Since the bounty hunter has no "constitutional safeguards" or "police standards or guidelines" to worry about, he is able to say and do things to elicit the information that a police officer cannot do.

Building a File

It is surprising the number of fugitives who live within fifty miles of their original residence after jumping bail. Most find it very difficult to sever all ties with their community, loved ones, and personal belongings.

The bondsman will give you as much information as he has on the individual. This will usually consist of a copy of the bond agreement and possibly a booking sheet from the local jail. Usually the first place to go after getting the contract is to introduce yourself to the local warrants officer at the county jail, or city jail if you are in a large city. Also, visit the police department and ask for the warrants officer.

In any case, let him know you are interested in the case, mention the bondsman's name and ask for any assistance he can give. Most of this information can be released as public, and the police agencies often do this for TV stations and the print media. Make a request for the same courtesy. Some items of information, however, are protected by the Privacy Act.

If you are lucky, you will get a photograph of the fugitive, usually a xerox. Begin to develop your own "rap sheet." Start logging all the information you can get on your man. Create a letter-size file for all information. You must be organized.

Armed with the paper you have and the authority to arrest (you should have a certified copy of the bail agreement and a power of attorney from the bondsman and whatever else your state demands), visit the fugitive's home. This will give you your first "sense" of the chase. Your target is now more than just a name on paper; he is a reality.

If the place is vacant and he was the last tenant, check with the landlord. Finding the landlord is easy as most title companies in all cities have a service where you just call in and ask for the owner of a certain listed address. The title service will tell you. Title companies can be found in the telephone book Yellow Pages.

Did the fugitive leave a forwarding address with the postal service? He might have if he was expecting some special mail. The postal authorities will pass this information on to you for about a dollar. Check with the window clerks for the procedure. Or you may simply mail a letter to the fugitive with the notation on the envelope in the lower left-hand corner: Address Correction Requested: Do Not Forward.

Assuming you contact the landlord, tell him you have a bill to present to the subject or that you are a long-lost cousin. Perhaps you can just level with the owner and tell him you are a "bail bond investigator." Don't use the term "bounty hunter." It draws a blank with most people and alarms the others.

Get as much information from the landlord as possible. Check the trash bin in the back of the house for any phone numbers or letters. Ask the landlord if you can get inside the house for a quick look.

Check with the neighbors. Do they know where your man went? Did they see him in a U-Haul truck or trailer? If so, check with the local outlet for these rental vehicles and see if there is a rental agreement. See if your subject's name is among the customers of the agency, and check the stated destination these agencies require. Of course, the owner of the agency should be helpful if you level with him.

Many skip tracing books will tell you to get the fugitive's driving record or his criminal record from the state's computer sources. Generally, these services are not available to the public, and this will include you.

This is where it helps to have sources. Getting your man's driving record is fairly easy if you know anybody working in an insurance office that has the CAIR plan. It may have a different name in various states, but basically this is a computer system whereby a person's Motor Vehicle Record (MVR) is sent to the requesting office— usually within a day. You need to get the name and driver's license number, for sure, and in some cases, the date of birth (DOB).

Getting your subject's criminal record from the state is an altogether different matter. Unless you have a contact within some police department, this is going to be almost impossible. The Privacy Act limits who can see these records. In any case, this may not be much help in your quest.

Military records can be had from the Military Personnel Records Center, 9700 Page Blvd., St. Louis, MO 63132. I know of individuals who have written to the address in question requesting information as if he were the fugitive. All you need is the fugitive's serial number or Social Security number and a sample of his handwriting. A DD 214 will be sent to you outlining the fugitive's military background, if he has one.

If your man is a Union Shop worker, it pays to check with the Union Hall in the city you are searching. This

Surveillance is a time-consuming part of bounty hunting; as much as 90 percent of a bountyman's time is spent in skip tracing and watch-

ing activities. Here Burton and a partner wait for a fugitive to show.

may be the first place he will turn up if he is on the run. Usually, most fugitives have little money and have to continue working, stealing, dealing, or whatever they do to earn bucks.

It is amazing the amount of information you can get from agencies if you pose as the subject himself. Getting your MVR direct from the records center may be easy if you approach it a few minutes to noon on a busy day. Tell them you are John Doe (the fugitive), and you have to have a copy of your MVR for an afternoon court appearance. If the clerk asks for your DL number, tell her the subject's number. Be sure to have that and the birthdate memorized. Do not fumble for a piece of paper in your pocket. If she asks to *see* your license, tell her to give you a break as you just came from the gym, and you don't have your wallet. You should anticipate this by dressing in jogging or gym clothes. It's always worked for me. Use the imagination I told you you'd need, and you'll get what you're going after.

Let's say three tickets turn up on the man's MVR in a town forty miles away. Why was he there and did he go there again to hide? These things are all part of the puzzle.

Just asking questions of everybody who knows him and is willing to talk will turn up one lead and then another. Usually these leads will be nothing but a dead end. Yet one will be the golden key. The main thing to remember is not to be discouraged. Patience is the glue that holds your operation together. Within a few weeks your file will be thicker, and you should go into an in-depth review of everything you have collected.

Profile of a Jumper

In developing a profile of a jumper, I turned to the major surety companies that write bail bonds. Surprisingly, I had no luck in getting any statistics. So, the following is sort of an "official bounty hunter's view" of bail jumpers. It is the result of interviewing several individuals involved in bounty hunting, law enforcement, and bondsmen.

Gypsys are sure (well, almost sure) to jump bail. I don't mean the settled businessman of Eastern European descent with a Gypsy heritage; but I am talking about people with a Gypsy background who never settled down. They can be found reading palms, running concessions at fairs, and sometimes dealing in bunco and auto fraud.

Other groups will flee just as readily of course. In the Los Angeles area, we have the Israeli "Mafia," the Iranian "Mafia," and various other ethnic criminal groups. Often feeding on legitimate businessmen of their own kind, they use terror, blackmail, and vandalism (much worse in some cases) to collect fees. Invariably many of these individuals will flee to their homelands if arrested and released on bail. Ralph Thorson has arranged for at least three to be brought back from Israel.

Mexican nationals in the U.S. either on a visa or illegally will split to Mexico or to some of the more "Mexican" parts of the U.S. such as Brownsville, Texas, the lower Rio Grande Valley, or various border towns. Many, however, will return to their native Mexican state.

Hookers, drug dealers, and others who have access to false identification will jump almost all the time. In San Francisco, posting bail is financially dangerous.

Bikers generally are not a big problem, especially if they belong to an organized club like the Hells Angels. The club will often cosign the bail agreement and guarantee the appearance of the defendant. Should he jump before his appearance, the bondsman will inform the club chieftain, and lo and behold, the miscreant will be in court on his appointed day . . . minus a few teeth.

Heavy dope dealers (not cocaine) will often jump. Apparently coke dealers have the bucks for good attorneys and high bail.

December seems to be the month for the highest percentage of jumps. Maybe it's the thought of going to a hearing or jail with "Silent Night" playing outside that drives so many people to jump. So, I think, is the specter of paying money to a defense attorney when the kids and the old lady should have something for Christmas.

An actual and statistically correct profile seems to elude us at this point. As I mentioned earlier, the above is the result of a good ol' boy session with some people who would be in a position to know. I must caution, however, that this not-quite-scientific profile is based on experience in Southern California. Why don't you attempt to develop a jumper's profile for your locale?

Creatures of Habit

Usually a fugitive changes his address and job but seldom his lifestyle. He or she may still like Chinese food, fast cars, avant garde movies, or low-class (or high-class) bars that show Monday Night Football. Anything that the man has done in past years, he generally can be expected to continue doing. Was he a printer in your town? Chances are he will seek the same occupation in a distant city. Fugitives have to work, and they prefer doing what they know best. Check the print shops, and don't be afraid to show his picture to those you talk to.

I have caught two fugitives by advertising for their specific skill in a newspaper of a town I suspected they were in. The compensation was high, so the investment in time, advertising and a rental office was worth it.

Relatives of the fugitive are often a big help. If they are average-citizen type people, they will find what the fugitive did distasteful. More than likely one or two relatives will offer to help, especially if the fugitive is dragging children or a wife along with him. I will appeal to the relatives' sense of righteousness or family to obtain their help. And as in the case of any source of information, you must promise on your word (and definitely mean what you say) *never* to disclose the source of any information you get.

Remember that all the while you are out in the field gathering this type of intelligence, you are also making repeat calls to the landlord, friends, and employers to see if they have heard anything. You have to continually work all your sources. This is an ever on-going and a must-do part of skip tracing.

Hitting It Lucky

Sometimes the most bizarre ploys must be used to gather information on a fugitive. In one situation I was involved in, we had had the subject's house under surveillance for over a week with no luck. We suspected he was there, as the woman he lived with was recognized as the party leaving every day to go to work. That someone was inside was evident from the shades going up and the wisp of smoke coming from the chimney.

We didn't want to alarm the fugitive and risk a fight, so we decided to pay a visit to the house posing as Jehovah's Witness solicitors. We went downtown and found a familiar Witness passing out the church's newspaper called *Awake.* I gave him five dollars for twenty of them and headed back to the house with an adventuresome woman I know. We were dressed conservatively and acted accordingly. The plan was that he would see us working the street across from him, and then watch us come up his side of the block. (Fugitives are always looking out a window.)

My male partner was in a delivery van in the driveway next door. The cue was that when I got to his door and he answered, if I recognized him, I would drop my load of booklets, bend down to pick them up, then rush the knees of the target. My female partner was to back off as I didn't want her to get involved, and at the same time, my male partner was to rush to the house.

As soon as he opened the door, I knew he was the fugitive. When you stare at someone's photo for months on end, something mystical pinches you when you actually confront the man, despite physical changes such as weight, beard, glasses, and different hair coloring.

I gave the fugitive my best rendition of "Brother, we are here to save you." He gave me an incredulous look and was about to slam the door when I dropped the papers on his side of the door sill. When I bent down to retrieve them, I heard a whack and realized that my female partner had punched him in the mouth. I was on his knees by now and could feel him tumbling backward. I knew that my awkward position would get me into trouble if my friend didn't get there in seconds.

The woman was still hitting the fugitive on the head as he struggled to get into position in the living room we had fallen into. Mike, my working partner, came in with a roar and threatened to smash the fugitive if he didn't stop struggling. He sighed one big sigh of resignation and simply went limp.

We had yelled "You're under arrest!" in order to get him to stop struggling. Many fugitives think they are being mugged or rolled unless you identify yourself. Often they cease struggling since they don't want to compound their troubles by "resisting arrest." In this case, the ploy worked well and unusually fast. It isn't always like that.

Conclusion

Skip tracing is an art and skill, a science and artistry. It is something that only time in the field will help you with. Yet if you are blessed with a good imagination, you will be miles ahead of the game.

To cover skip tracing completely in this section of the book would be impossible. A book this size or more would be necessary. But I suggest these two books as very valuable assets:

Tracing Missing Persons
by Michael Zoglio
89 pages; $14.50 postpaid
Tower Hill Press
PO Box 1132
Doylestown, PA 18901

Skip Tracing
by Bob Stephenson
25 pages; $25
c/o Bob Stephenson
PO Box 2111
Monterey, CA 93940

Skip tracing books can be found at local collection agencies and some libraries. The agencies will at least let you get the publisher's name and address. To recap in Bob Stephenson's words, "Remember that when there is a piece of information somewhere, there is a way to get it!"

6. Contacts: An In

THE MOST IMPORTANT KEY IN bounty hunting is the "contact" that puts you onto the tail or address of the bail jumper. These contacts or "snitches" are the essential assets in any bounty hunter's arsenal. Snitches can be fellow dope dealers who want the bail jumper put away and out of competition or the buyer he angered in some way. Wives or girlfriends often sell out their husbands or boyfriends for money. This is especially so when their relationship is one of monetary support rather than deep love. Mothers have told me where to find their bail-jumping sons so "he won't have to run the rest of his life." In general, snitches sing to the tune of money if they know where a man is.

In all cases, when I ask a snitch for the whereabouts of a bail jumper, I offer money. Let's say the commission on a certain bail is $2,000. I'd offer a snitch up to $200 for valid information leading to my capturing the jumper. The snitch mostly knows that unless you get your man he won't get paid. If he doesn't know, or you're not sure if he does, make damn sure you tell him so: no prisoner no cash. The last thing you want is a snitch spreading the word that you welch on your promises.

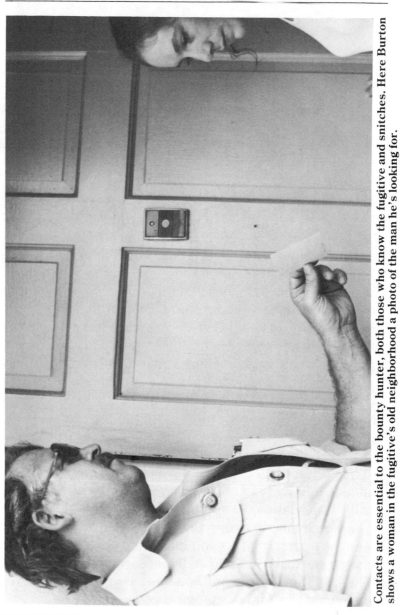

Contacts are essential to the bounty hunter, both those who know the fugitive and snitches. Here Burton shows a woman in the fugitive's old neighborhood a photo of the man he's looking for.

Taxi drivers seem to know what's happening in a town more than the average person. When tracing a jumper to a small or medium-sized city, I often write down on a small file card the details of what I need in the way of information and print the word "reward." This serves as incentive to the drivers to keep their eyes open for a certain type of car or the mention of a jumper's name or description.

Suppose you are given a contract to pick up a bail jumper and your fee is $4,000. Wouldn't it be nice to be able to pick up the phone, make six or seven calls, and find out the subject's address, the make of the car he is driving, and his work address?

That's what snitches and contacts are for. These people aren't the chamber-of-commerce or banking-type guy. They border on the criminal—maybe as heavy dope or cocaine users, ex-felons, former police officers, or cabdrivers, bartenders, waitresses, etc. in rough areas. These people generally know who has been arrested, who has been released, who has jumped bail, and who is about to. They have their finger on the pulse, so to speak, of the city's criminal element. These people are your contacts.

Don't overlook, however, the friendly telephone lineman or operator, answering service employees, and cable-television installers. These people have access to records you might need. Sit down and develop a list of friends you have, and people you should court as friends and the jobs they have that place them in positions of access.

You'll want friends and contacts having access to all kinds of lists: telephone, gas hookups, mail delivery, various city, county and state institutions, motor vehicle departments, etc. Look for anyone with access and the desire to sell you information. And don't be afraid to offer to buy this information for ten to fifty dollars a throw.

As you get more experience and respectability, the local police will help you. Cooperate with the detective working on the same case. Exchange information with him. You will have to make the first move until he gets to know you. If you develop a new lead in the pursuit of your man, share it with the police.

Remember, however, that if the police pick your man up first, you have lost a paycheck. Generally the average detective may have a load of ten, twenty, or more cases he is working on. He won't be able to work on finding one man as much as you can.

Contacts will be of two general kinds: case contacts and community contacts. While the terminology is strictly mine, I think other bounty hunters will agree. A *case contact* is one who is directly related to the jumper you are looking for, and I don't necessarily mean blood relatives. Case contacts could be the jumper's upset mother-in-law who doesn't like her daughter running around with a bail jumper or his uncles, parents, friends, former employers, or anyone who knows the jumper of your pursuit.

Community contacts, on the other hand, are those individuals who have access to the rumors in the street. These are often bartenders, waitresses, and just "street people." While they might not know the individual personally or closely, they know "of" him and his whereabouts. They can be bribed, bought, or cajoled to pass on information to you. Many of these people are curious about bounty hunters and will help for no other reason than to be part of the "romance" of the whole thing. Encourage them.

Some of my better contacts in the past were a couple of kids who worked in a pizza place. They seemed to know everybody who had problems with the law, yet they themselves were certainly noncriminal. I'm not sure how they came to know about this nineteen-year-old would-be cocaine dealer I was looking for, but they did. And when I found him working as a gardener at an "old folks' home," it turned out to be one of the more colorful failures I have had as a hunter.

My partner Bill and I went to the home at a time we knew our man was going to be there. Sure enough, there he was, wearing hip boots and giving the hedges their early morning water. I approached him and told him we had some mulch to sell and asked his name. Something to the effect of "Tom" is what he told us, although our man was named, or nicknamed "Tab." I dropped the pretense of the mulch and asked him for his I.D.

"Sure, hold this," he said, and he passed the running hose to me.

Like an idiot, I accepted it in time to see him rev up into a sprint that would do justice to the Olympics as he disappeared down the walkway with my partner right behind him.

As Tab passed an outdoor garden table, the heavy metal type with an umbrella coming out of a hole in the center, he reached out and grabbed the umbrella, pulling the whole thing down as Bill reached the spot. Bill missed being hit but slipped on the wet cement and slid into a pile of garbage cans. Tab disappeared between two glass doors into the rest home. Three seconds later, a squat, drill-instructor-type head nurse came out bellowing, "What the hell is going on here?"

I could see Tab about fifty feet down the hallway inside. I also saw all these frail white heads, raising in a ghostly all-white setting, to peer out at us.

Brushing past the hollering head nurse, Bill took off into the building after Tab, and I raced to the front in case he went for the front door. As I got to the front lobby, Bill was coming down the hallway. Old folks on wheeled stretchers were startled, nurses were staring at both of us, and the head nurse was running after Bill, frantically pumping her shorter, heavier legs while trying to maintain decorum. All the while, she was yelling, "Hey you, who are you? What the hell's going on here?"

Without a word, Bill and I shot up a flight of stairs and out onto the roof. We found our man's rubber hip boots neatly placed on the edge of the one-story building. He had jumped below and run up a creek bed to his freedom. We lost seven hundred bucks and gained some skinned knees. We also got out of the rest home in a hurry before someone called the police. At least I take comfort in knowing that we provided some excitement for those old folks. They're probably still talking about it.

7. The Pick Up

FINDING AND TAKING YOUR MAN into custody is the most thrilling event in the bounty hunting process. It is also the most dangerous. There is no way I can cover all aspects of this particular fact of the operation in this book. But here are some helpful suggestions.

I have used everything from staging a phony bicycle accident with the fugitive's car to posing as a landlord to get inside the jumper's house. I have walked up behind my targets in bars and dragged them to the floor, and I have confronted them outside a mini-market with a gun. The circumstances of each pickup have 1,001 variations; no one can tell you how to arrange for them. Experience will be your teacher there.

In most cases, no violence is necessary. I have put my hand on very big men and felt all their energy and strength drain out when I told them they were under arrest. If I had to come up with a figure, I would say that fewer than 25 percent resisted. And that figure depends on how many (if any) of their friends were handy, how much drugs or booze they had in them, and the situation, i.e., crowds, Christmas Eve, etc.

Burton pats down two jumpers for weapons while Ralph Thorson keeps them from making threatening moves, at top. Below, Burton handcuffs each man, snapping the cuffs on the left wrist first.

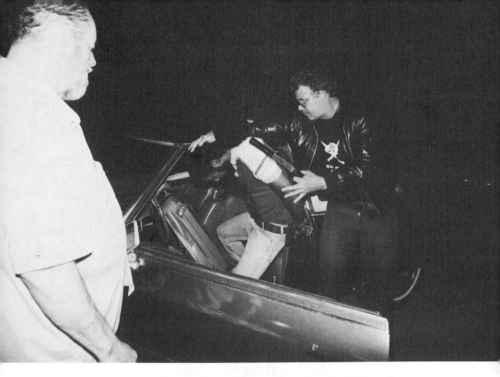

Into the car they go for a trip to the precinct, handcuffed *and* seat-belted into place, at top. Below, Burton keeps an eye on them. The bounty hunter must have a copy of the bail agreement when he turns a fugitive in. Without authorization to arrest from the bondsman, the bounty hunter is nothing more than a kidnapper.

In many cases, I have had no photo of the subject and have had to rely on description and traits. In several situations, I have had to stage some event where I could get the subject to identify himself to me. One case involved a small time crook who liked to take his clothes off on public beaches and snort cocaine. He always carried a knife, however, and street talk had it that wouldn't hesitate to use it.

His major crime, however, was that he had failed to appear in court and had jumped bail. It was only a small bail, and my commission was to be only $600. Since he lived nearby, or so I hoped, it was worth the effort, however; after all, six hundred bucks is six hundred bucks.

The target lived in the student community surrounding San Luis Obispo, California's university. I had a new man with me who wanted to get involved in the business. He was a former Marine, intelligent, and weighed 320 pounds which made for good muscle. We introduced ourselves to the watch commander of the University Police late one evening. Bounty hunters have no real identification per se other than a business card. But I have an ID card from a New York bonding company that I used to do an occasional pickup for.

I showed the watch commander a certified copy of the bail agreement as well as some copies of booking sheets from the county jail. Satisfied that I wasn't just a noisy bill collector and that I could do him a favor by getting rid of one more problem, he jumped at helping us.

It seemed he had quite a file on our man: address, job, previous arrests, and lots of pictures which I didn't have.

I went over the address given me by the campus police officer and parked my car in the shadow of a man-sized hedge. It was roughly 11 P.M., but the streets were full of people, dogs, and bicyclists. Stereo music came from all the apartments, and it was a balmy September night in California.

My friend started to move around to the rear of the apartment, a duplex. Because of our sizes and ages, we in no way looked like students just passing through. Plus my friend, on his first operation with me, dressed up like the Guns of Navarone team: black turtleneck, black watch cap, and black pants. The only thing missing was black face makeup.

I was looking for a name on a mail box when I heard a voice asking, "Can I help you?"

I told this unwanted-intruder I was looking for Lynn Hynes (our target) to offer him some work, as I was a friend of his father's. The student said he needed work, and could I use him? I told him yes, but I had a moral obligation to Hynes' father to ask Hynes first. I then asked the kid if he knew what apartment our man was in, and he pointed a few feet away to an upstairs apartment and said, "Yeah, right there, and he's there now. His light is on."

I had bad vibes and was in no mood to go into the kid's apartment. On calm analysis I can't figure out why I didn't; it was just a gut feeling. The big Marine and I went back to the car and figured out what to do next. I had given the photo back to the campus officer, so all I had in memory was a mug shot taken of our man about a year ago. The last thing I wanted to do was grab the wrong man and get involved in a wrongful arrest situation.

To make a long story short, my big Marine and I spent the night in the car half sleeping and half watching our target's apartment. The next morning we were joined by my partner who wanted to be in on the pickup for no other reason than that he had nothing else to do that morning. By 9:30 A.M., our man had not come out. I decided

Having kicked in a door, Burton charges a fugitive he knows is unarmed. The impact gun gives him just enough time to handcuff his subject.

to go in posing as the landlord with the big Marine as my painter and tell them that we were going to paint the apartment.

I walked up the single flight of steps to the porch and found four people sitting in the living room. I knocked briskly, and since the door was open, sort of invited myself, in saying, "Hello, landlord here."

One of the kids, bright and cheerful, came over and introduced himself to me and so did the next one. I coached the next one into introducing himself until finally one unidentified man was left.

He looked up and I said, "Hi, what's your name?"

"Lynn."

"What's your last name Lynn?"

"Hynes. Lynn Hynes."

My adrenaline started about that time. "Well, Lynn, how about giving me a hand to bring up the painting equipment?"

The four students were ecstatic about a new paint job. Hell, the place had Day-Glo paint all over it. Lynn walked to the balcony, and I yelled to my other partner, still in the car, to bring the paint up. As Bill approached the steps below in a blocking position, I grabbed the target and informed him of his arrest for jumping bail. Simultaneously my Marine placed his 320 pounds between my back and the other three in the apartment.

Everybody was in shock. In this not-too-criminal element, everyone figured we were plain-clothes officers. We slipped cuffs on our man and immediately frisked him down. Finding nothing, we hustled him off to our car. We sat him in the right rear seat, and the Marine sat beside him. We put the seat belt on him for extra security and/or restraint.

I found out later that the kids in the apartment went over to the campus police and complained about the "sneaky police tactics." The police informed them that we were bounty hunters and that we did nothing illegal. And rightly so.

Nothing was really special about this operation; it was more routine than not. I only use it to illustrate the typical pickup. No shootouts; no giant fist fights; no sexy blondes, bribes, or intrigue; just a lot of questions.

I must stress, however, that it only takes one foul up—one wrong move—with a really dangerous person to finish your career. I have had more cars aimed at me than guns, more guns than I care to count and lots of fists thrown (and too many connections).

I can't tell you how to pick your man up, per se; that's where your imagination comes in. I can tell you, however, how to handle him once you've got him.

Always work with a partner, preferably one you've spent quite a lot of time with and with whom you enjoy good communication. Map out your plans in advance, including plans for contingencies. For instance, what if the guy decks you? What if he takes off inside his home or apartment house, maybe for a gun? Or what if his buddies take one glance at what's going on and decide they hate you? Decide in advance when you'll hold and when you'll run. Always plan an escape route in case things escalate more quickly than you can handle.

Read a couple of good police tactics books and watch how the "officers" handle TV pickups. Of course, you won't kick in a door and then stand in the doorway. You won't stand against a background where you can easily be picked off by a hostile gunman. Keep a low profile. Remember that in some neighborhoods where you'll be traveling, your fugitive won't be the only person you'll have to fear; the color of your skin or the make of your car may be enough for someone to decide to eliminate you.

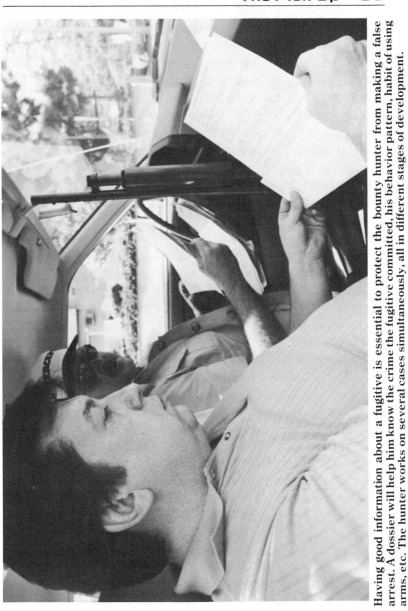

Having good information about a fugitive is essential to protect the bounty hunter from making a false arrest. A dossier will help him know the crime the fugitive committed, his behavior pattern, habit of using arms, etc. The hunter works on several cases simultaneously, all in different stages of development.

You'll never walk into a room where you don't know pretty much what you can expect. And if at all possible, you'll approach your subject in such a way that you'll have the element of surprise on your side. Don't give him time to gather his courage or make quick mental plans before you nab him. I try to avoid a fight at all cost, simply because I prefer not to be even "slightly" injured by a flying fist or foot. And if the situation looks like it's escalating to the point of "get-your-man-or-die-trying," I'll definitely back away from the "die-trying" aspect of it. My accountant tells me that the return from a job isn't too good if I have to spend three weeks recovering from a beating, unable to work.

As I have alluded to before, at the instant of pickup, maintain your authority and bark the phrase, "You're under arrest." Few fugitives will resist once they *know* they've been nabbed in the name of the law. However, *never* impersonate an officer.

Your first objective is to get handcuffs on your man. You want his arms securely locked behind his back. If he's down on account of a scuffle, lock the cuffs on him then. But if he isn't resisting you, have him lean against a wall or car with his feet three or so feet out to keep him off balance. While your partner covers you, pat down the fugitive to check for weapons (or contraband he might not want to be caught with if you want to be kind). Check him good; you don't want any surprises.

Then handcuff him by taking first his left arm and bringing it behind his back. Snap the cuff on. Then get his right arm, put it behind him, and snap the cuff closed.

Put the fugitive in the rear seat on the passenger's side. Your partner can ride back there with him to keep him honest on the way to the precinct station. But more about this in the transporting chapter.

So you have a screaming, vomiting, kicking, or spitting individual in the back seat. You now must take him to the precinct station where his warrant was issued. In my area I know the warrants officer and regularly exchange information with him. It is very important to assist these officers in any way you can if you want any help from them. I often call ahead and tell the WO we are bringing someone in so the paperwork will be ready.

When we arrive at the county jail, we take the prisoner to the holding cell just adjacent to the booking area. There he is searched and booked. If you don't want to embarrass yourself, make damn sure you search him thoroughly after you pick him up. In one of my first cases, I failed to search the man and the sheriff's deputies found a boot knife, a buckle knife, and marijuana pipes.

I often find dope on my fugitives, and they are all grateful when I suggest throwing it away or giving it to a friend, if one is present. They don't need any more charges when the booking process begins.

Leave some respect with your just-arrested man. It's not necessary to harass him, call him names, punch him, or anything else. If the arrest can be done quietly and without alarming anybody, do it. I'm not talking about the heroin-selling sleaze-bag who has jumped his fifth assault charge; take him fast and hard. But most people aren't like that. They've fallen afoul of the law by simply not being willing to face up to the charges. A good percentage may eventually be found innocent. But they jump bail, pissing off the bondsman and putting into financial jeopardy the person who signed as collateral for them.

In California, we can only keep the fugitive in custody forty-eight hours after the pickup. If the forty-eight hours end on a weekend, you can turn him in Monday morning. If you have brought your man back to California from

On cases the bounty hunter knows will involve violence, he should call for help. Here Ralph Thorson brings in his man with the help of the local police. Being "coward" enough to want to protect himself keeps a bounty hunter alive long enough to enjoy his profits.

another state, you have forty-eight hours after entering the state to turn him in. But more on state laws later.

When I arrive at the jail, I always tell the jailer if the prisoner is an asshole or if he's compliant. It helps the jailer, and the prisoner will appreciate it if he's behaving himself.

8. Bribes

A COUPLE OF SUMMERS AGO I WAS working a case with a well-known bounty hunter from Southern California named Mike Johnson. Johnson, one of those guys who operates by instinct, was working on a case about a Newark, New Jersey, "torcher." This arsonist had fled to San Diego from a sizable bond in Massachusetts. We knew his girlfriend owned a string of boutiques in the San Diego coastal area and had them under surveillance. Finally we had a good lead from a snitch in the apartment house complex where she lived: our arsonist was living with her.

Staking out the apartment one Friday night, we discovered our man was in the apartment next door at a party. Knowing a pickup was imminent, I notified a local station of the San Diego P.D. They had cooperated with us earlier and asked us to call them if we found him. I think it was out of curiosity that the watch commander wanted to come along.

When I got back to Johnson, he informed me that our man had gone back to his apartment. We didn't want to bust him in the middle of a party not knowing his relationship with the other participants. And with the party so close to the fugitive's apartment, it was just as well that two uniformed officers arrived.

We waited a few more hours in the darkness of a doorway for the party to wind down. The commander stayed with us while the other officer was in the car. About 10:30 P.M., we decided to go in.

The fugitive's apartment had been black since he entered almost two hours earlier. Mike and I approached the door and knocked. I was off to the side, Mike was at an angle to the door, and the two officers were in the background. There was no answer to our repeated knocks, yet we knew he had to be there unless he had gone out a back window.

The younger officer said we could keep the place under surveillance, and he would come back in the morning with a search warrant. Before I could reply, Johnson said, "Oh Bulllllshiiit!" and threw his weight against the door, crashing into the room with me in tow. Not knowing if our man had a bead on us in the darkness, we spread out immediately but heard no shots. The door to the bedroom was open, and on first glance no suspect was to be seen. We flicked lights on and cautiously searched the house. We found our man, almost shaking in fear, behind the shower curtain in the tub.

His first words were to the effect of "Don't take me! Don't take me! I'll give you $10,000!" Hmmmmmm. . . .

Yet we cuffed him up and took him out to our car. We never even discussed his offer until a few weeks later. Ironically, we never got paid for this operation as the bonding company went bankrupt shortly after the pickup, leaving us high and dry.

In your work, you will be offered bribes by men who are about to lose their freedom. Don't even *think* of taking them. Your personal honor, your reputation, and the possibility of your breaking the law are at stake.

Not only would you be morally and ethically incorrect to accept a bribe, but you would jeopardize your future if the fugitive was later picked up and bragged about buying you off.

On taking bribes: don't even think about it.

On giving bribes: think twice about it. Make certain that you'll be getting your money's worth. That old saying that money talks is certainly true. But try to arrange it so that you hand over your bribe *after* the subject has talked. That way, you'll both be getting what you want.

In towns south of the border, a bribe called "mordida" is, in fact, expected before you'll get any cooperation. Just remember that while you can get what you want and need with bribery, you can easily be taken, too.

Plan a certain amount of money into your expense account on each case for greasing the wallets of contacts and Mexican police if your work takes you there. You can find that in some instances, it will be the best money you ever spent.

9. Prisoner Transport

WHAT IS MORE IMPORTANT THAN getting your man or woman to jail? Yet plans for transporting can be overlooked. I heard of a bounty hunter who did his work in an Austin Healy in the Sacramento, California, area. Putting a big prisoner next to you in a car like that can be damn dangerous.

Ideally, I feel the car should be a four-door equipped with restraining devices on the floor in the back to restrain the feet of the prisoner. Remember, the handcuffs are situated so that his arms are held *behind* him. You have your partner next to him in the rear and someone is driving.

A van is perfect for interstate deals and long rides within your state. Equip it with a portable toilet, some shackles, and a ring on the floor, and you can transport a prisoner in style. A mattress on the floor will provide comfort enough for the prisoner for a three-day ride. Give him a brisk walk once every tankful of gas or whenever you feel it necessary. Attach regular hardware-store chain to the cuffs to prevent your man from running; yes, even with cuffs on, he can run. With the chain you can walk him as if he's on a leash. And going back to my earlier words on the subject of respect. Should this situation arise, don't make light of it by referring to walking a dog. Your prisoner may be under extreme stress, and the situation will be distasteful enough as it is.

Airplanes offer the easiest and fastest prisoner transport, but they have one major drawback; the handcuffs must come off so the prisoner can save himself should the plane crash.

Below are some guidelines that have come into usage among some airlines. These airlines have both their own regulations and those of the federal government which are listed under Federal Air Regulations (FAR) under codes 108.21.

Eastern Airlines:

• When making reservations, inform the reservation agent that you will be escorting a prisoner. This should be done as early as possible.

• A single prisoner must be accompanied by two guards. If more than one prisoner is being transported, the number of guards must exceed the number of prisoners by one.

• When changing airlines enroute, you must book separate reservations with each airline since many airlines may have minor procedure differences.

• Your prisoner must be handcuffed, but not chained. (This statement came from Eastern. Maybe Eastern allows handcuffed prisoners.)

• Guards must maintain control of the prisoner at all times. Guards are not allowed alcohol while on the flight. Guards should position themselves between the prisoner and the aisle of the aircraft. If possible, guards and prisoners should board the aircraft first and deplane last.

United Airlines:
• United Airlines policy is that of the Federal Aviation Regulations which will follow.

PSA:
• Only one "maximum risk category" prisoner will be allowed. Maximum risk includes but is not limited to murder, terrorists, etc. and two escorts must be available.

• Arrangements must be made prior to boarding. The prisoner and escorts will board before the other passengers. Prior to boarding, the escorts will advise the station agent that they are escorting a prisoner. The station agent will advise the pilot of the prisoner's and guards' seat locations. The guards and prisoner will be assigned the rearmost seating location other than seats adjacent to normal or emergency exits or on the aisle.

• At least one guard will be seated between the aisle and the prisoner's seat. Should the prisoner use the lavatory, the guard must keep the door open for surveillance. The guards and prisoner shall remain seated until all passengers have left the plane.

American Airlines:
Call American before buying tickets and ask for the "Acceptance Coordinator" for specific instructions. Generally the rules should be similar to the other airlines.

Federal Aviation Regulations 108.21
(a) Except as provided in paragraph (e) of this section, no certificate holder (airline) required to conduct screening under a security program may carry a passenger in the custody of armed law enforcement escort aboard an airplane for which screening is required unless:

1. The armed law enforcement escort is an official or employee of the United States or political subdivision of a state or a municipality who is required by appropriate authority to maintain custody and control over an individual aboard an airplane;

2. The certificate holder (airline) is notified by the responsible government entity at least one hour or, in case of emergency, as soon as possible before departure (i) of the identity of the passenger to be carried and the flight on which it is proposed to carry the passenger; and (ii) whether or not the passenger is considered to be in a maximum risk category;

3. If the passenger is considered to be in the maximum risk category, that the passenger is under the control of at least two armed law enforcement escorts and no other passengers are under the control of those two law enforcement escorts;

4. No more than one passenger . . . in a maximum risk category is carried on the airplane;

5. If the passenger is not considered to be a maximum risk category, the passenger is under the control of at least one armed law enforcement escort and no more than two of these persons are carried under the control of any one law enforcement escort;

6. The certificate holder (airline) is assured, prior to departure, by each law enforcement escort that (i) The officer is equipped with adequate restraining devices to be used in the event restraint of any passenger under the control of the escort becomes necessary; and (ii) Each passenger under the control of the escort has been searched and does not have on or about his or her person or property anything that can be used as a deadly or dangerous weapon;

7. Each passenger under the control of a law enforcement escort is (i) Boarded before any other passengers when boarding at the airport where the flight originates and deplaned at the destination after all other deplaning passsengers have deplaned; (ii) Seated in the rearmost passenger seat when boarding at the airport where the flight originates; and (iii) Seated in a seat that is neither located in any lounge area nor located next to or directly across from an exit.

8.(a) A law enforcement escort having control of a passenger is seated between the passenger and any aisle.

(b) No certificate holder (airline) operating an airplane under paragraph (a) of this section may

1. Serve food and beverage or provide metal eating utensils to a passenger under the control of a law enforcement escort while aboard the airplane unless authorized to do so by the law enforcement escort.

2. Serve a law enforcement escort or the passenger under the control of the escort any alcoholic beverages while aboard the airplane.

(c) Each law enforcement escort carried under the provisions of paragraph (a) of this section shall, at all times, accompany the passenger under the control of the escort and keep the passenger under surveillance while aboard the airplane.

(d) No law enforcement escort carried under paragraph (b) of this section or any passenger under the control of the escort may drink alcoholic beverages while aboard the airplane.

There are several key words in this section. One is the word "law enforcement escort." A bounty hunter would not qualify as this. As a result, handcuffs would have to be taken off. The subject would have to be taken on the plane uncuffed. I personally feel that a bounty hunter armed with a certified copy of bail and a power of attorney could qualify under the second paragraph as one ". . . who is required by appropriate authority to maintain custody and control over an individual aboard an airplane." I have hassled this point with the FAA several times, and it's still up in the air.

Read these laws several times and do your own thinking. The more you know about this business the better and safer you will be.

Women Prisoners

If that subtitle sounds like the title of a cheap movie, it's not! It's the fact of this business that you will have to pick up a woman who jumped bail. This situation can be touchy, very touchy. If people see two men with a struggling woman, there is some fiction in their minds that says "rape." Bounty hunters can't whip out police badges and identify themselves and the fact that they are making a lawful arrest. And what angry crowd is going to sit still while you try to explain the U.S. Penal Code as it pertains to bail bond arrest?

If you must arrest a woman, bring along another woman to soften the harshness of the arrest. This will only pay off if the subject resists arrest, which you can never foresee. Most will come peacefully.

I have found that meter maids can be very useful. While most are not sworn police officers, they carry a police identification card and, in some cases, a badge. You must have a woman with you who is willing to help you physically subdue the subject. Just having a woman on the scene is not enough. She should be bigger than average size and physique if you feel the subject will resist arrest. Otherwise, a woman of average height is fine.

My male partner and I had one lousy experience when we brought a woman jumper to California for a San Diego bondsman. We picked her up in Valdosta, Georgia, and our intention was to drive straight through to San Diego with her in our van. Unfortunately, we found out that she had a very unpleasant habit of throwing her excrement at us. We had a porta-pottie rigged up for her, and twice she heaved the stuff at us. We had to take her to a farm house, and give the farmer $25 so we could use his hose to wash her and the van down. Not relishing twenty-five hundred miles of travel with a shit thrower, we boarded a plane in New Orleans for a few hours' journey to San Diego.

Transporting prisoners is a critical factor in a small percentage of pickups. It certainly is in those involving interstate pickups. With a woman aboard, it can be damn sensitive. I would have been tempted to belt a guy throwing excrement about my van; but delivering a woman to county jail with a fat lip and black eyes would be too touchy.

While we're on the subject of transport, let me mention that your car should be used for transporting the fugitive to the police station and not as a weapon for battering nor as a vehicle for high-speed chases. Both can get you into *far* more trouble than the reward of bringing the prisoner in would be worth.

Full speed car chases are the stuff movies are made of. Yet when they occur, the ride can be scarier, riskier and probably more expensive for the bounty hunter than for the fugitive. The one big chase I had was in Tijuana, Mexico, some years ago. We were looking for a Mexican national jumper for the San Diego bondsman who posted his bail.

After a two-month fruitless hunt, we got a tip he was working at a relative's restaurant on one of Tijuana's side streets. After we waited outside for four hours one hot July afternoon, our man came out of the front door and got into a very beat up '51 Ford "convertible," which was simply an ordinary coupe with the roof cut off. We pulled alongside his car to block it but no such luck with this macho hombre; he simply turned the wheels inward and drove up on the sidewalk to the accompaniment of screams, twisting metal signs and screeching rubber. Any studio would have loved to have had this for stock footage.

Everybody in Tijuana seemed to be looking in our direction. Yet we had no choice but to proceed (although in hindsight, it seems foolish as the bounty was only $75 apiece). Running parallel to him we followed him to the corner where he jumped off the curb onto El Revolucion Boulevard. At that time the main street, called El Rev, was half dirt and two-thirds potholes. As our culprit hit the street, dust, smoke, and four hub caps went in all directions. A very startled Tijuana police officer standing in the middle of the street directing traffic jumped about ten feet and went for his pistola.

In the crosswalk, our man made a sharp right and headed down into town at which we headed north, muy pronto. At that time, the Mexican police were all over Tijuana handling the Marines and U.S. Navy personnel who came down there to raise hell and drink some 35-cent tequilla. The payment for a night of fighting (assuming no Mexican nationals were too banged up) was a $35 fine and a night in la carcel (jail). If the troublemakers were military personnel, it meant double trouble if the MPs had to come—usually Captain's Mast, fines, and confinement.

But we were bounty hunters down in Tijuana to kidnap a Mexican citizen and drag him across the border.

We also had weapons in the car and that was a "no no." Our problems would have been much greater if we were arrested.

When I say headed north, it was actually a broadside turn through the intersection, hub caps flying and further startling the Mexican traffic officer. This had turned into a Hail Mary operation.

I was driving scared. My partner was yelling "Go! Go! Go!" and I was. I must have run five traffic lights (two of which were working). I almost hit a line of cars waiting to get through the Mexican Customs stop on the Mexican side. However, I controlled my panic. I started blowing my horn and slid, speeding, through the gap between the lined-up cars on the left and the pottery hawkers on the right side. All I could see was a blur of bright colors and all I could hear was the horn.

In those days, the Tijuana police had no reservations about shooting, and we were concerned about that. The bridge was just ahead, and we were still out of control (thankfully). Over the bridge and dead ahead was U.S. Customs at San Ysidro.

We literally forced our way into U.S. Customs much to the startlement of the border patrolmen. My car was leaking oil badly from one wheel when I realized I was out of breath. I simply had not taken a breath in the estimated five minutes it took to get to the border, at least not a deep breath.

Explaining our problem to the Captain in charge of the INS, we found a not too sympathetic ear. Of course, he had no authority to surrender us to the Mexicans, either. We were sent on our way after we filled out some forms detailing the incident.

I have since picked up five individuals in Mexico in far smoother operations. I always, however, have a drink of tequilla at the restaurant where the chase began twenty-three years ago.

10. Bail Arrest Laws

IT IS *VERY* IMPORTANT THAT YOU know the laws pertaining to bail arrest in any state you operate in. These laws can generally be found in the law books of any good-sized library within the state, certainly within the courthouse law library of each county seat. Every attorney has a set of his state's laws within his office walls.

The section that usually carries bail arrest information can be found in the Index of all law book series. It is listed under Bail.

Under this section the reference words are usually "Surrender of Defendant by Bail."

Other laws might pertain to your pursuit of an individual, such as laws covering carrying a weapon, carrying a concealed weapon, or covering you as an out-of-state bounty hunter. This means that when you go into California from Arizona hunting for an Arizona bail jumper, you had best be aware that the bail arrest laws are different. Most bail arrest laws pertain to a particular state, for example, an Arizona bail bondsman using an Arizona bounty hunter to look for an Arizona bail jumper in Arizona. If the Arizona bounty hunter arrests the Arizona bail jumper in Los Angeles, he *may* have violated California law which states that an out-of-state bondsman must pick up a warrant in a municipal court before arresting the jumper.

That's what the law *states*. The fact of the matter is that it is seldom followed. In fact, a recent ruling (*Ouzts* v. *Maryland Nt. Ins. Co.*) held that the arrest of a California resident by a Nevada bounty hunter did not violate any right guaranteed to the bail jumper by the constitution or federal law and was not a basis for a civil rights suit.

Use these laws as the key to any state's bail arrest laws. Consult a friendly bondsman for additional reading.

I have no intention of passing as the final word on up-to-date bail arrest laws. It is up to each and every individual to keep himself apprised of changes in bail arrest codes. Most of these laws have not changed in years. It isn't like they are in a constant state of flux.

The very necessity of knowing these laws, coupled with your temperament, demeanor and appearance might —just might—result in a bondsman giving you a contract. Remember, the bondsman, by giving you an endorsed certified copy of the bail agreement, could open himself up to a lawsuit if you did not act with the proper "discretion" that so many codes and laws state is necessary.

The bondsman is not looking for a bruiser. He is looking for a three-hundred pound linebacker with the wit and wisdom of Plato, the temperament of Woody Allen, the nose of Pluto, and the mind of F. Lee Bailey. Impossible dream? Perhaps, but there are many who approach this business who think all you have to do is man-handle the fugitive into the back seat of a car and hustle him off to the slammer.

Better start by knowing the laws.

WARNING

The following section on the state laws pertaining to Bail Arrest is from a modern legal library with an up-to-date filing system for law books. This does not preclude error on the part of the law book publishing house, the library, or this author.

The final word on state Bail Arrest laws should be your own research in your own city's library.

Alabama

From: Criminal Procedure Code

15-13-62. Exoneration of bail by surrender of defendant prior to conditional judgment; bail may arrest or authorize arrest of principal

"Bail may, at any time before a conditional judgment is entered against them, exonerate themselves by surrendering the defendant; and for that purpose, they may arrest the defendant on a certified copy of the undertaking at any place in the state, or may authorize another person to arrest him by an endorsement in writing on such copy."

Alabama has traditionally given wide latitude to bondsmen to arrest their principals. Also read the following codes in the same section: 15-13-63 Arrest of defendant by bail after conditional judgement; and 15-13-64 surrender of defendant to sheriff required to exonerate bail; when new bail allowed.

Alaska

From: Alaska Statutes

Section 09.40.200 Arrest of Defendant by or on authority of bail

"For the purpose of surrending the defendant, the bail, at any time and place before they are finally charged, may personally arrest the defendant, or, by a written authority endorsed on a certified copy of the undertaking, may empower a peace officer to do so. Upon the arrest of the defendant by a peace officer, or upon delivery of the defendant to the peace officer by the bail, or upon the defendant's own surrender, the bail are exonerated if the arrest, delivery or surrender takes place at a time before judgment. But if the arrest, delivery or surrender does not take place before judgment, the bail are finally charged on their undertaking and bound to pay the amount of the judgment."

Sections following and preceding this particular section are to be read as well.

Arizona

From: Criminal Code

13-3885 Arrest of principal by surety

"For the purpose of surrendering the defendant, a surety on the bail bond of defendant may arrest him before the forfeiture of the undertaking, or by written authority endorsed on a certified copy of the undertaking, may empower any adult person of suitable discretion to do so."

Arizona's law pertaining to bail arrest is simple and straightforward. It is based on the Model Code of Criminal Procedure and adopted by the U.S. Supreme Court. (See Code 1939, 44-102 et seq.)

Arkansas

From: Criminal Procedure

43-716 Surrender of defendant—right of bail

"At any time before the forfeiture of their bond, the bail may surrender the defendant, or the defendant may surrender himself, to the jailer of the county in which the offense was committed; but the surrender must be accompanied by a certified copy of the bail-bond to be delivered to the jailer, who must detain the defendant in custody thereon as upon a commitment, and give a written acknowledgment of the surrender; and the bail shall thereupon be exonerated."

This is a law very similar to those used in California, Idaho, Mississippi, and seven other states.

43-717 Authority to surrender

"For the purpose of surrendering the defendant, the bail may obtain from the officer having in his custody the bail-bond or recognizance, a certified copy thereof, and thereupon at any place in the State arrest the defendant, or by his written indorsement thereon, authorize any person over the age of twenty-one (21) to do so."

43-718 Authority to make arrest

"The bail may arrest the defendant without such certified copy."

While the two above codes may seem at odds regarding the need for a certified copy, there is a slight difference. Code 43-718 states the bail "may arrest the defendant without such certified copy"; the other code states the bail "may obtain" a certified copy for the purpose of surrendering his charge. Without second guessing Arkansas authorities, it would appear the certified copy would be necessary for surrender of the charge and not necessarily a must for the act of arrest.

My suggestion is to take an Arkansas bail bondsman to a long and wet lunch, and don't be cheap.

California
From: Penal Code
1301 Arrest by bail or depositor for purpose of surrender

"For the purpose of surrendering the defendant, the bail or any person who has deposited money or bonds to secure the release of the defendant, at any time before such bail or other person is finally discharged, and at any place within the state, may himself arrest defendant, or by written authority indorsed on a certified copy of the undertaking or a certified copy of the certificate of deposit, may empower any person of suitable age to do so.

Any bail or other person who so arrests a defendant in this state shall, without necessary delay, and, in any event, within forty-eight hours of the arrest, deliver the defendant to the court or magistrate before whom the defendant is required to appear or to the custody of the sheriff or police for confinement in the appropriate jail in the county or city in which defendant is required to appear. Any bail or other person who arrests a defendant outside this state shall, without unnecessary delay after the time defendant is brought into this state, and, in any event, within forty-eight hours after defendant is brought into this state, deliver the defendant to the custody of the court or magistrate before whom the defendant is required to appear or to the custody of the sheriff or police for confinement in the appropriate jail in the county or city in which defendant is required to appear.

Any bail or other person who willfully fails to deliver a defendant to the court, magistrate, sheriff, or police as required by this section is guilty of a misdemeanor.

. . . The provisions of this section relating to the time of delivery of a defendant are for his benefit and, with the consent of the bail, may be waived by him. To be valid, such waiver shall be in writing, signed by the defendant, and delivered to such bail or other person within forty-eight hours after the defendant's arrest or entry into this state, as the case may be. The defendant, at any time and in the same manner, may revoke said waiver. Whereupon, he shall be delivered as provided herein without unnecessary delay and, in any event within forty-eight hours from the time of such revocation.

If any forty-eight hour period specified in this section terminates on a Saturday, Sunday or holiday, delivery of a defendant by a bail or other person to the court or magistrate or to the custody of the sheriff or police may, without violating this section, take place before noon on the next day following which is not a Saturday, Sunday or holiday."

Colorado

From: Criminal Proceedings
16-4-108 Exoneration from bond liability.

(1) Any person executing a bail bond as principal or as surety shall be exonerated as follows:

(a) When the condition of the bond has been satisfied; or

(b) When the amount of the forfeiture has been paid; or

(c) Upon surrender of the defendant into custody at any time before a judgment has been entered against the sureties for forfeiture of the bond, upon payment of all costs occasioned thereby. A surety may seize and surrender the defendant to the sheriff of the county wherein the bond is taken, and it is the duty of the sheriff, on such surrender and delivery to him of a certified copy of the bond by which the surety is bound, to take the person into custody and, by writing, acknowledge the surrender. If a compensated surety is exonerated by surrending a defendant prior to the appearance date fixed in the bond, the court, after a hearing, may require the surety to refund part or all of the bond premium paid by the defendant if necessary to prevent unjust enrichment.

"(2) Upon entry of an order for deferred prosecution as authorized in section 16-7-401, sureties upon any bond given for the appearance of the defendant shall be released from liability of such bond."

Connecticut
From: Criminal Procedure and Bail
54-65 Surety may surrender his principal

"Any surety in a recognizance in criminal proceedings, who believes that his principal intends to abscond, may have the same remedy, and proceed and be discharged in the same manner, as sureties upon bail bonds in civil actions."

This is not quite as definite in language as some of the other states but still authority enough. In "Notes of Decisions" following this section, the often used *Taylor* v. *Taintor* decision of the Supreme Court is used. This is the decision most often used in defense of Bail's arrest rights. It is the quote on the first page of this book.

Delaware
From: Superior Court Criminal Rules: Rule 46
Rule 46. Bail

Extracted "(g) Exoneration: When the condition of the bond has been satisfied or the forfeiture thereof has been set aside or remitted, the Court shall exonerate the obligors and release any bail. A surety may be exonerated by a deposit of cash in the amount of the bond or by a timely surrender of the defendant into custody. (Amended, effective June 1, 1969; May 10, 1973.)"

District of Columbia

This is a federal district and bail is administered by federal commissioners. Check with local authorities for regulations.

Florida

From: Criminal Procedure

903.21 Method of surrender; exoneration of charges

"(1) A surety desiring to surrender a defendant shall deliver a certified copy of the bond and the defendant to the official who had custody of the defendant at the time bail was taken or to the official into whose custody he would have been placed if he had been committed. The official shall take the defendant into custody, as on a commitment, and issue a certified acknowledging the surrender.

(2) When a surety presents the certificate and a certified copy of the bond to the court having jurisdiction, the court shall order the obligors exonerated and any money or bonds as bail refunded. The surety shall give the prosecuting attorney three days notice of application for an order of exoneration and furnish him a copy of the certificate and bond.

903.22 Arrest of principal by surety before forfeiture

"A surety may arrest the defendant before a forfeiture of the bond for the purpose of surrendering him or he may authorize a peace officer to make the arrest by indorsing the authorization on a certified copy of the bond."

Check with a Florida bondsman on his definition of "peace officer." According to notes on this law by one legal publishing house, the bondsman may "deputize a peace officer" in order to seize the principal.

Georgia

From: Criminal Procedure
27-904 Surety surrendering principal; forfeiture proceedings; death of principal.

"A surety on a bond may surrender his principal in open court or, when the court is not in session, to the sheriff in order to be released from liability. If the principal does not appear by the end of the day on which the principal was bound to appear, forfeiture proceedings shall be initiated. The death of the principal shall be equivalent to a surrender."

27-904 Bail surrendering principal; costs; death of principal

"Bail may surrender their principal in vacation to the sheriff, or in open court, in discharge of themselves from liability, and such privilege shall continue to the last day of the term, without liability for costs for a forfeiture of the bond. After forfeiture, and before final judgment, the bail may, at any time, surrender their principal, upon payment of all costs accruing up to that time. The death of the principal at any time before final judgment shall be equivalent to a surrender, and the court shall, after final judgment, relieve the sureties of the penalty of the bond upon surrender of the principal and payment of the costs."

Hawaii

From: Procedural and Supplementary Provisions
804-41 Discharge of surety.

"At any time before the breach of the conditions of the bond, the surety may discharge himself by surrendering the principal into the hands of any sheriff or the chief of police or his authorized subordinate."

Idaho

From: Criminal Procedure

19-2924 Surrender of defendant by bail

"At any time before the forfeiture of their undertaking, the bail may surrender the defendant in their exoneration, or he may surrender himself to the officer in whose custody he was committed at the time of giving bail in the following manner:

1. A certified copy of the undertaking of the bail must be delivered to the officer, who must detain the defendant in his custody thereon as upon a commitment, and by a certificate in writing acknowledge the surrender.

2. Upon the undertaking and the certificate of the officer, the court in which the action or appeal is pending may, upon notice of five (5) days to the prosecuting attorney of the county, with a copy of the undertaking and a certificate, order that the bail be exonerated, and on filing the order and the papers used on the application, they are exonerated accordingly.

19-2925 Arrest of defendant for surrender

"For the purpose of surrendering the defendant, the bail, at any time before they are finally discharged, and at any place within the state, may themselves arrest him, or by written authority endorsed on a certified copy of the undertaking, may empower any person of suitable age and discretion to do so."

Illinois

Illinois has many laws hostile to the act of bail arrest. Tolerance towards and acceptance of bail arrest vary from county to county. Check locally.

Indiana

35-1-22-7(9-1036) Surrender of principal

"When a surety on any recognizance desires to surrender his principal, he may procure a copy of the recognizance from the clerk, by virtue of which such surety, or any person authorized by him, may take the principal in any county within the state."

35-4-5-5(9-3728) Surrender of defendant—forfeiture of bond premium

"At any time before there has been a breach of the undertaking in any type of bail and cash bond the surety may surrender the defendant, or the defendant may surrender himself to the official to whose custody the defendant was committed at the time bail was taken, or to the official into whose custody the defendant would have been given had he been committed. The defendant may be surrendered without the return of premium for the bond if he has been guilty of changing address without notifying his bondsman, conceals himself, or leaves the jurisdiction of the court without the permission of his bondsman or the court, or of violating his contract with the bondsman in any way that does harm to the bondsman, or the surety or violates his obligation to the court."

35-4-5-6(9-3729) Certified copy of undertaking to accompany surrender—release from liability—refund—

"The person desiring to make a surrender of the defendant shall procure a certified copy of the undertakings and deliver them together with the defendant to the official in whose custody the defendant was at the time bail was taken, or to the official into whose custody he would have been given had he been committed, who shall detain the defendant in his custody thereon, as upon a commitment, and by a certificate in writing acknowledge the surrender.

Upon the presentation of certified copy of the undertakings and certificate to the official, the court before which the defendant has been held to answer, or the court in which the preliminary examination, indictment, information or appeal, as the case may be, is pending, shall upon notice of three (3) days given by the person making the surrender to the prosecuting officer of the court having jurisdiction of the offense, together with a copy of the undertakings and certificate, order that the obligors be exonerated from liability of their undertakings; and, if money or bonds have been deposited as bail, that such money or bonds be refunded."

35-4-5-6 Arrest of defendant before surrender

"For the purpose of surrendering the defendant, the surety may apprehend him before or after the forfeiture of the undertaking, or by written authority endorsed on a certified copy of the undertaking may empower any law-enforcement officer to make apprehension, first paying the lawful fees therefor."

Iowa

From: Criminal Procedure
811.8 Surrender of defendant

"1. At any time before the forfeiture of the undertaking, surety may surrender the defendant, or the defendant may surrender himself or herself, to the officer to whose custody was committed at the time of giving bail, and such officer shall detain the defendant as upon a commitment and must, upon such surrender and the receipt of a certified copy of the undertaking of bail, acknowledge the surrender by a certificate in writing.

2. Upon the filing of the undertaking and the certificate of the officer, or the certificate of the officer alone if money has been deposited instead of bail, the court or clerk shall immediately order return of the money deposited to the person who deposited the same, or order for exoneration of the surety.

3. For the purpose of surrendering the defendant, the surety, at any time before finally charged and at any place within the state, may arrest the defendant, or, by a written authority endorsed on a certified copy of the undertaking, may empower any person of suitable age and discretion to do so."

Kansas
From: Criminal Procedure
22-2809 Surrender of obligor by surety

"Any person who is released on an appearance bond may be arrested by such surety or any person authorized by such surety and delivered to a custodial officer of the court in any county in the state in which he is charged and brought before any magistrate having power to commit for the crime charged; and at the request of the surety, the magistrate shall commit the party so arrested and indorse on the bond, or a certified copy thereof, the discharge of such surety; and the person so committed shall be held in custody until released as provided by law."

Kentucky

From: Rules of Criminal Procedure, Bail IV

RCr 4.50 Surrender of defendant; exoneration

"(1) At any time before forfeiture, any surety may procure a certified copy of the bail bond which shall authorize any peace officer to whom it is presented to arrest the defendant in any county within the Commonwealth and to deliver him and the certified copy of the bail bond to the jailer in the county in which the prosecution is pending. The jailer shall acknowledge the surrender in writing.

(2) Upon presentation of the writing executed by the jailer, the court before which the defendant has been held to answer shall, after five (5) days notice to the county attorney, order that the surety or sureties be exonerated from liability on the bond or recognizance and that any money or bonds that have been deposited as bail be returned to the person making the deposit."

Note: Kentucky has passed many laws unfavorable to the bail bond industry. Check locally for updated information on any matter pertaining to bail arrest.

Louisiana

From: Code of Criminal Procedure

Article 338 Surrender of defendant

"A surety may surrender the defendant or the defendant may surrender himself to the officer charged with his detention, at any time prior to forfeiture or within the time allowed by law for setting aside a judgment of forfeiture of the bail bond. Upon surrender of the defendant, the officer shall detain the defendant in his custody as upon the original commitment, and shall acknowledge the surrender by a certificate signed by him and delivered to the surety. Thereafter the surety shall not be responsible for the defendant."

Article 340 Arrest of defendant by surety
"For the purpose of surrendering the defendant, the surety may arrest him."

Maine
From: Criminal Procedure
852. Responsibility of sureties
"All sureties shall be responsible for the appearance of their principal at all times until verdict, unless said sureties have sooner surrendered him into the custody of the sheriff or jailer of the county in which the case is pending."

Maryland
From: Maryland Rule 722(h).

(The Maryland Rules are promulgated by the Court of Appeals pursuant to Maryland Constitution Article IV, Section 18 which provides that the rules have the force of law.)

"h. Voluntary Surrender of Defendant by Surety

A surety into whose custody a defendant has been released upon the execution of a bail bond may procure the discharge of the bail bond at any time before forfeiture of the bond by:

(i) delivery of a copy of the bond and refund of any fee, premium or compensation stated therein to the court in which the charges are pending who shall thereupon issue a commitment of the defendant to the custodian of the jail or detention center; and

(ii) delivery of the defendant and the commitment to the custodian of the jail or detention center, who shall thereupon issue a receipt for the defendant to the surety.

Unless the defendant is released on a new bond, he shall be taken forthwith before a judge of the court in which the charges are pending. The court may, upon the petition of the surety or any person who paid the fee, premium, or compensation, and after notice and opportunity to be heard, order that portion thereof to be returned to the surety the court determines should be allowed the surety for his expenses in locating and surrendering the defendant, and direct that the balance be refunded to the person who paid it."

Massachusetts

From: C.276 Annotated Laws of Massachusetts

68 Surrender of principal before default; return of certificate, new bail

"Bail in criminal cases may be exonerated at any time before default upon their recognizance by surrending their principal into court or to the jailer in the county where the principal is held to appear, or by such voluntary surrender by the principal himself, and in either event, in all cases where bank books, money or bonds are deposited by the surety, the court shall thereupon order the bank books, money or bonds so deposited to be returned to the surety or his order, and to be reassigned to the person entitled thereto. They shall deliver to the jailer their principal, with certified copy of the recognizance, and he shall be received and detained by the jailer, but may again be bailed in the manner as if committed for not finding sureties to recognize for him, provided that the surety making the surrender shall not be accepted as bail if the person surrendered shall again be bailed. The jailer shall forthwith notify the clerk or justice of the court where the proceeding is pending of such surrender."

This is one of the more wordy and oddly written statues.

Michigan

From: Code of Criminal Procedure

765.26 Release of surety; arrest of accused; mittimus

"Sec. 26. In all criminal cases where any person or persons have entered into any recognizance for the personal appearance of another and such bail and surety shall afterwards desire to be relieved from his responsibility, he may with or without assistance, arrest the accused and deliver him at the jail or to the sheriff of said county. In making such arrest he shall be entitled to the assistance of the sheriff, chief of police or any city or any peace officer. The sheriff or keeper of any jail in said county is authorized to receive such principal and detain him in jail until he is discharged in due course of law.

Upon delivery of his principal at the jail by the surety or any officer, such surety shall be released from the conditions of his recognizance. Whenever the prosecuting attorney of any county shall become satisfied that any person who has been recognized to appear for trial has absconded, or is about to abscond, and that his sureties or either of them have become worthless, or are about to dispose or have disposed of their property for the purpose of evading the payment or the obligation of such bond or recognizance, or with intent to defraud their creditors, and such prosecuting attorney shall make a satisfactory showing to this effect to the court having jurisdiction of such person, said court or judge shall forthwith grant a mittimus to the sheriff or any constable of said county, commanding him forthwith to arrest the person so recognized and bring him before the officer issuing such mittimus, and on the return of said mittimus may, after a full hearing on the merits, order him to be recommitted to the county jail until such time as he shall give additional and satisfactory sureties, or be otherwise discharged according to law."

Minnesota

From: Criminal Procedure
629.63 Surrender of principal; notice to sheriff
"When a surety for any person held to answer, upon any charge or otherwise, shall believe that his principal is about to abscond, or that he will not appear as required by his recognizance, or not otherwise perform the conditions thereof, he may arrest and take such principal, or cause him to be arrested and taken, before the officer who admitted him to bail, or the judge of the court before which such principal was by his recognizance required to appear, and surrender him up to such officer or judge; or any such surety may have such person arrested by the sheriff of the county by delivering to him a certified copy of the recognizance or instrument of bail under which he is held as surety, with a direction to such sheriff, endorsed thereon, requiring him to arrest such principal and bring him before such officer or judge to be so surrendered, and on the receipt thereof, and a tender or payment to him of his fees therefor, such sheriff shall arrest such principal and bring him before such officer or judge, to be so surrendered. Before any surety shall personally surrender such person, the sheriff shall be notified, and he or one of his deputies be present to take him into custody if he shall fail to give new bail as herein provided."

Mississippi
From: Criminal Procedure
99-5-27. Sureties may arrest and surrender defendant

"Bail may, at any time before final judgment, surrender their principal, in vacation to the sheriff, or in open court, in discharge of their liability; but if this be done after forfeiture of the bond or recognizance, the breach of the bond or recognizance must be satisfactorily excused before the court, and all costs be paid by the bail, and such part of the bond or recognizance as the court orders. Upon surrender, the sheriff in vacation, and the court in term-time, may discharge the prisoner on his giving new bail, but if he does not give new bail, he shall be detained in jail. Bail may arrest their principal anywhere or authorize another to do so."

99-5-29. Surety may cause arrest of principal by officer

"The sheriff or a constable in a proper case, upon the request of a surety in any bond or recognizance, and tender of the legal fee for executing a capias in a criminal case, and the production of a certified copy of the bond of recognizance, shall arrest within his county, the principal in the bond or recognizance. The surety or his agent shall accompany the officer to receive the person."

Missouri
From: Arrest, Examination, etc.
544.600. Surrender of principal, how made

"When a bail desires to surrender his principal, he may procure a copy of the recognizance from the clerk, by virtue of which the bail, or any person authorized by him, may take the principal in any county within this state.

544.610. Discharge of bailor's liability, how made

"The bailor at any time before final judgment against him upon a forfeited recognizance, may surrender his principal in open court or to the sheriff; and upon the payment of all costs occasioned by the forfeiture, and all costs that may accrue at the term to which the prisoner was recognized to appear, may thereupon be discharged from any further liability upon the recognizance.

544.620. What deemed a surrender

"The bailor must deliver a certified copy of the recognizance to the sheriff with the principal, and the sheriff must accept the surrender of the principal, and acknowledge such acceptance in writing."

Montana

From: Criminal Procedure
46-9-205. Surrender of defendant

"(1) (a) At any time before the forfeiture of bail, the defendant may surrender himself to the officer to whose custody he was committed at the time of giving bail.

(b) At any time before the forfeiture of bail, the sureties or surety company may surrender the defendant to the officer to whose custody he was committed and for this purpose may themselves arrest the defendant or by written authority endorsed on a certified copy of the undertaking may empower any person of suitable age and discretion to do so.

(2) The officer must detain the defendant in his custody as upon commitment and shall file a certificate in the court having jurisdiction of the defendant acknowledging the surrender. Such court may then order the bail exonerated."

Nebraska

From: Criminal Procedure

29-905. Bail; Surrender of accused by surety to court; discharge of surety; new recognizance.

"When any person, who is surety in a recognizance for the appearance of any defendant before any court in this state, desires to surrender the defendant, he shall, by delivering the defendant in open court, be discharged from any further responsibility on such recognizance; and the defendant shall be committed by the court to the jail of the county, unless he shall give a new recognizance, with good and sufficient sureties in such amount as the court may determine, conditioned as the original recognizance."

29.906. Bail; surrender of accused by surety to sheriff; authority.

"In all cases of bail for the appearance of any person or persons charged with any criminal offense, the surety or sureties of such person or persons may, at any time before judgement is rendered against him or them, seize and surrender such person or persons charged as aforesaid to the sheriff of the county wherein the recognizance shall be taken."

Nevada

From: General Provisions

178.526 Sureties may arrest and surrender defendant

"For the purpose of surrendering the defendant, the sureties, at any time before they are fully discharged, and at any place within the state, may themselves arrest him, or by written authority, endorsed on a certified copy of the undertaking, may empower any person of suitable age and discretion to do so."

New Hampshire
From: Proceedings in Criminal Cases
608:10 Committal by Surety
"A surety, in a recognizance to keep the peace, may commit the principal to the common jail, and shall be discharged in the same manner as sureties in other recognizances in criminal cases."

New Jersey
From: Civil Actions, Generally—Arrest and Bail
2A: 15-47 Render in discharge of bail
"The defendant may, on notice to the plaintiff, render himself or be rendered in discharge of his bail, either before or after judgment, to the court in which action was brought; but such render shall be made within 20 days after proceedings or an action is commenced against the bail on the recognizance of bail and not after, unless for good cause the court grants further time. Upon the render the defendant shall be committed, and thereupon the bail shall be discharged. At any time before judgment in the action, a defendant who has been rendered in discharge of his bail or has been arrested as provided in section 2A:15-44 of this title, may be released on again giving bail, on notice to the plaintiff."

New Mexico
31-3-3. Surrender of principal by surety
"A. When a surety desires to be discharged from the obligation of its bail bond, the surety may arrest the accused and deliver him to the sheriff of the county in which the action against the accused is pending.
B. The surety shall, at the time of surrendering the accused, deliver to the sheriff a certified copy of the order admitting the accused to bail and a certified copy of the

bail bond. Delivery of these documents shall be sufficient authority for the sheriff to receive and retain the accused until he is otherwise bailed or discharged.

C. Upon the delivery of the accused as provided in this section, the surety may apply to the court for an order discharging him from liability as surety; and upon satisfactory proof being made that this section has been complied with, the court shall enter an order discharging the surety from liability.

D. This section shall not apply to a paid surety as defined by Section 31-3-4 NMSA 1978."

31-3-4. Paid Sureties

"A. A "paid surety" is a surety that has taken money, property or other consideration to act as a surety for the accused.

B. When a paid surety desires to be discharged from the obligation of its bond, it may arrest the accused and deliver him to the sheriff of the county in which the action against the accused is pending.

C. The paid surety shall, at the time of surrending the accused, deliver to the sheriff a certified copy of the order admitting the accused to bail and a certified copy of the bail bond. Delivery of these documents shall be sufficient authority for the sheriff to receive and retain the accused until he may be brought before the court.

D. A paid surety may be released from the obligation of its bond only by an order of the court.

E. The court shall order the discharge of a paid surety if: (1) there has been a final disposition of all charges against the accused; (2) the accused is dead; (3) circumstances have arisen which the surety could not have foreseen at the time it became a paid surety for the accused; or (4) the contractual agreement between the surety, the principal, and the state has terminated."

New York

From: Special & Misc. Proceedings

530.80 Order of recognizance or bail; surrender of defendant

"1. At any time before the forfeiture of a bail bond, an obligor may surrender the defendant in his exoneration, or the defendant may surrender himself, to the court in which his case is pending or to the sheriff to whose custody he was committed at the time of giving bail, in the following manner:

(a) A certified copy of the bail bond must be delivered to the sheriff, who must detail the defendant in his custody thereon, as upon a commitment. The sheriff must acknowledge the surrender by a certificate in writing, and must forthwith notify the court in which the case is pending that such surrender has been made.

(b) Upon the bail bond and certificate of the sheriff, or upon the surrender to the court in which the case is pending, such court must, upon five days notice to the district attorney, order that the bail be exonerated. On filing such order, the bail is exonerated accordingly.

2. For the purpose of surrendering the defendant, an obligor may take him into custody at any place within the state, or he may, by a written authority indorsed on a certified copy of the bail bond, empower any person over twenty years of age to do so.

3. At any time before the forfeiture of cash bail, the defendant may surrender himself in the manner prescribed in subdivision one. In such case, the court must order a return of the money to the person who posted it, upon producing the certificate of the sheriff showing the

surrender, and upon a notice of five days to the district attorney."

North Carolina
From: Ch.85C. Bail Bondsman and Runners
85C-5. Surrender of defendant by surety; when premium need not be returned

"At any time before there has been a breach of the undertaking in any type of bail or fine and cash bond the surety may surrender the defendant to the official to whose custody the defendant was committed at the time bail was taken, or to the official into whose custody the defendant would have been given had he been committed; in such case the full premium shall be returned. The defendant may be surrendered without the return of premium for the bond if he has been guilty of nonpayment of premium, changing address without notifying his bondsman, concealing himself leaving the jurisdiction of the court without the permission of his bondsman or violating his obligation to the court."

85C-6. Procedure for surrender; exoneration of obligors; refund of deposit

(This section refers to procedure of procuring a certified copy of the bond and surrendering to the correct official)

85C-7. Arrest of defendant for purpose of surrender

"For the purpose of surrendering the defendant, the surety may arrest him before the forfeiture of the undertaking, or by his written authority endorsed on a certified copy of the undertaking, may request any judicial officer to order arrest of the defendant."

North Dakota
From: Rules of Criminal Procedure
Rule 46 Release from custody
"(h) Exoneration. If the condition of the bond has been satisfied or the forfeiture thereof has been set aside or remitted, the court shall exonerate the obligors and release any bail. A surety may be exonerated by a deposit of cash in the amount of the bond or by a timely surrender of the defendant into custody."

Ohio
From: Special remedies—Courts
2713-22 Bail may arrest defendant
"For the purpose of surrendering the defendant, the bail may arrest him at any time or place before he is finally charged, or, by a written authority indorsed on a certified copy of the bond, may empower any person of suitable age and discretion to do so."

Oklahoma
From: Criminal Procedure
1107. Arrest of defendant by bail—commitment of defendant and exoneration of bail
"Any party charged with a criminal offense and admitted to bail may be arrested by his bail at any time before they are finally discharged, and at any place within the state; or by a written authority indorsed on a certified copy of the recognizance, bond or undertaking, may empower any officer or person of suitable age and discretion, to do so, and he may be surrendered and delivered to the proper sheriff or other officer, before any court, judge or magistrate having the proper jurisdiction in the case; and at the request of such bail the court, judge or magistrate shall recommit the party so arrested to the custody of the

sheriff or other officer, and indorse on the cognizance, bond or undertaking or certified copy thereof, after notice to the county attorney, and if no cause to the contrary appear, the discharge and exoneration of such bail; and the party so committed shall therefrom be held in custody until discharged by due course of law."

Oregon

Oregon bail arrest laws are changing. Check with local bondsman or authorities.

Pennsylvania

From: Rules of Criminal Procedure 4016 and case law as in Bail, Key #80 of Pennsylvania Digest 2d.

Rule 4016. Breach of bail and forfeiture of bond; process and bail pieces; exoneration of surety.

A. Remedies on Breach

"(1) Forfeiture

(a) When a breach of a condition of bail occurs, the issuing authority or court may declare the bond forfeited and make a record thereof.

(b) Upon such declaration written notice of such forfeiture shall be given to the surety either personally or by certified mail at his last known address. When there is no surety such notice shall be given to the defendant at his last known address.

(c) The issuing authority or the court may direct that a forfeiture be set aside upon such conditions as may be imposed if it appears that justice does not require enforcement of the forfeiture.

(d) Execution on the bond may issue at the expiration of fifteen (15) days following notice.

(2) Warrants

(a) When a breach of a condition of bail occurs, the issuing authority or court may also issue an appropriate process to bring the defendant before it.

(b) Upon service of such process the defendant shall not thereafter be released upon bail except upon further order of the person who issued the process, or if he is unavailable, upon order of the president judge of the judicial district or the judge presiding in the criminal division of the court.

(3) Bail Pieces.

The surety may be a bail piece from the court. If the court is satisfied that a bail piece is required, it may issue a bail piece authorizing the surety to apprehend and detain the defendant whenever and wherever he may be found and to bring the defendant before the issuing authority or court without unnecessary delay.

B. Exoneration of Surety

A surety may be exonerated by a deposit of cash in the amount of any forfeiture ordered or by timely surrender of a defendant in custody. When the conditions of the bond have been satisfied or the forfeiture thereof has been set aside or remitted, the issuing authority or court shall exonerate the obligors."

(Volume 6, West's Pennsylvania Digest 2d)

Key 80—Surrender of principal

"C.A.Pa. 1971, A bondsman has the right to pursue his principal into a state other than the one where the bond was executed and arrest him for purpose of returning him to state from which he fled.

"D.C.Pa. 1971, Under common law, surety on bail bond or his appointed deputy may take his principal into custody wherever he may be found without process in order to deliver him to the proper authority so surety may avoid liability on bond, and so long as bounds of reasonable means needed to effect apprehension are not trangressed and purpose of recapture is proper in light of surety's undertaking, surety will not be liable for returning their principals to proper custody.

Pa.Common Pleas 1974, Where defendants whose bail had been ordered forfeited for nonappearance, subsequently voluntarily surrendered themselves, at least partly by reason of the efforts of their bondsman, without any expense to the county, the orders of forfeiture were vacated, and the amounts previously paid by the bondsman were ordered returned to him."

Rhode Island

From: Criminal Procedure

12-13-18. Power of surety on recognizance over principal

"Every person who shall be surety in any recognizance to keep the peace, or for the appearance of any person accused or of any witness, or in any recognizance which shall be given on claiming an appeal, shall have the same power and authority over his principal as though he were bail for him in any civil cause.

12-13-19. Surrender or commitment of principal

Such surety may at any time surrender his principal to the court or magistrate who took such recognizance; provided, that in case any recognizance shall have been certified to some other court, the surrender shall be made to such court when in session; or such surety may at any time commit his principal to the adult correctional institutions, leaving with the warden a certified copy of such recognizance; and upon such surrender or commitment, such surety shall be discharged and exempt from all liability for any act of the principal subsequent thereto, which would have been a breach of the condition of the recognizance."

South Carolina

From: Arrest and Bail in Civil Actions; Civil Remedies and Procedures

15-17-730. Surrender of defendant

"At any time before a failure to comply with the undertaking the bail may surrender the defendant in their exoneration or he may surrender himself to the sheriff of the county in which he was arrested in the following manner:

(1) A certified copy of the undertaking of the bail shall be delivered to the sheriff or constable who shall, by a certificate in writing, acknowledge the surrender; and

(2) Upon the production of a copy of the undertaking and the sheriff's or constable's certificate a judge or clerk of the court may, upon notice to the plaintiff of eight days with a copy of certificate, order that the bail be exonerated.

And on filing the order and papers used on such application they shall be exonerated accordingly. But this section shall not apply to an arrest for the cause mentioned in item (2) of 15-17-20, so as to discharge the bail from an undertaking given to the effect provided by 15-69-140."

15-17-740. Bail may authorize arrest of defendant

"For the purpose of surrendering the defendant the bail, at any time or place before they are finally charged, may themselves arrest him or by a written authority endorsed on a certified copy of the undertaking may empower any power of suitable age and discretion to do so."

South Dakota

From: Criminal Procedure

23A-43-29 Arrest of defendant by surety on violation of conditions—recommitment and discharge of surety

"Any defendant who is released on the execution of an appearance bail bond with one or more sureties may, if he violates the conditions of his release, in vacation, be arrested by his surety, delivered to a law enforcement officer, and brought before any committing magistrate. At the request of such surety, the committing magistrate shall recommit the defendant to the custody of the law enforcement officer, and endorse on the recognizance, or certified copy thereof, the discharge and exoneretur of the surety. The person so committed shall be held in custody until discharged by due course of law."

Tennessee

From: Criminal Procedure

40-11-133 Arrest of defendant by bail

"For the purpose of Section 40-11-132, the bail may arrest the defendant on a certified copy of the undertaking, at any place in this state, or may, by a written authority endorsed on such copy, authorize another person to make the arrest.

40-11-134 Sheriff assisting bail in arrest

They are also entitled to the aid of the sheriff of any county in this state in making the arrest within the bounds of his county, by producing a certified copy of the bail bond, and, in person or by agent, accompanying said officer to receive the person arrested.

40-11-135. Return of bail bond after arrest

The sheriff making the arrest under section 40-11-134 shall return the copy of the bail bond, with an endorsement of his action, in the same manner as he is required to return a capias.

40-11-136. Surrender to sheriff

The surrender shall be made to the sheriff of the county in which the defendant is bound to answer for the offense, whether by change of venue or otherwise, and such sheriff is not bound to accept the surrender unless made at the place of holding the court in said county, or at the sheriff's residence, or the county jail."

Texas

From: Code of Criminal Procedure; Bail

Article 17.16 (282) (330) (318) Surety may surrender his principal

"Those who have become bail for the accused, or either of them, may at any time relieve themselves of their undertaking by surrendering the accused into the custody of the sheriff of the county where he is prosecuted."

Utah

From: Utah Code of Criminal Procedure

77-20-8. Continuation of bail on conviction—surrender of defendant—arrest of defendant by surety

(1) Upon conviction, by plea or trial, the court may order a defendant to be taken into custody or may order the bail continued pending imposition of sentence. The sureties may, at any time prior to a forfeiture of their bail, surrender the defendant and obtain exoneration of their bail by filing written requests therefor at the time of the surrender.

(2) To effect surrender, a certified copy, in duplicate, of the undertaking shall be delivered to a peace officer, who shall then detain the defendant in his custody as

upon a commitment, and who shall in writing acknowledge the surrender upon one copy of the undertaking. This certified copy of the undertaking upon which the acknowledgement of surrender is endorsed shall be filed with the court. The court may then, upon proper application, order the undertaking exonerated and may order a refund of any premium paid, or any part thereof, as it deems just.

(3) For the purpose of surrendering the defendant, the sureties, at any time before they are finally exonerated and at any place within the state, may arrest him."

Vermont

From: Vermont rules of criminal procedure
Rule 4.3

Note: this rule was formerly covered under section 3480 and 3481. These sections allowed discharge of the surety on mesne process by delivery of the defendant into court. These were considered merely declaratory of the common law. Essentially, the bail had the defendant on a string and could pull the string at his pleasure and surrender the defendant in discharge of the undertaking.

See the Washington State section for similar common law powers. Verify with Vermont bail bondsman as procedure may vary slightly.

Virginia

From: Criminal Procedure
19.2-149. How surety in recognizance may surrender principal and be discharged from liability

"A surety in a recognizance may at any time arrest his principal and surrender him to the court before which the recognizance was taken or before which such principal's appearance is required, or to the sheriff, sergeant, or jailer of the county or city wherein the court before which such principal's appearance is located; in addition to the above authority, upon application of the surety, the court, or the clerk thereof, before which the recognizance was taken, or before which such principal's appearance is required, shall issue a capias for the arrest of such principal, and such capias may be executed by such surety, or his authorized agent, or by any sheriff, sergeant or police officer, and the person executing such capias shall deliver such principal and such capias to the sheriff or jailer of the county or the sheriff, sergeant or jailer of the city in which the appearance of such principle is required, and thereupon the said surety shall be discharged from liability for any act of the principal subsequent thereto. Such sheriff, sergeant or jailer shall thereafter deliver such capias to the clerk of such court, with his endorsement thereon acknowledging delivery of such principal to his custody.

19.2-150 Proceeding when surety surrenders principal

If the surrender be to the court, it shall make such order as it deems proper; if the surrender be to a sheriff, sergeant or jailer, the officer to whom the accused has been surrendered shall give the surety a certificate of the fact. After such surrender the accused shall be treated in accordance with provisions of section 19.2-123 unless the court or judge thereof has reason to believe that no one or more conditions of release will reasonably assure that the accused will not flee or pose a danger to any other person or the community."

Washington

From: 8AmJur 2d Bail & Recognizance

Washington State has no statute covering Bail Arrest or Surrender of Defendant by Surety. The State of Washington operates under common law powers.

Section 119. Generally

"The sureties on a bail or recognizance are entitled to take the principal into custody for the purpose of surrendering him in exoneration of their liability. Such right has been likened to the rearrest by the sheriff of an escaping prisoner. But this right is not derived from the state through subrogation; it is an original right arising from the relationship between the principal and his bail. And the right exists in the case of a bail bond given on appeal from a conviction.

The right of bail in civil cases to arrest the principal is the same as in criminal cases.

Section 120. Delegation of authority

In the absence of statutory limitations, sureties on a bail bond may deputize others of suitable age and discretion to take the principal into custody. However, where a statute provides the manner in which the power of arrest may be delegated by the bail bondsman, that provision must be followed or the rearrest is invalid.

The person empowered by the bondsman to arrest the principal may not delegate his authority.

Where the surety on a bail bond procures the rearrest of his principal by a sheriff, or other peace officer, it is the general rule that the officer is empowered to make the arrest as an agent of the surety and not as an officer per se.

Section 121. Time of arrest

The right of sureties on a bail bond or recognizance to take their principal into custody for the purpose of surrendering him in exoneration of their liability may, in general, be exercised whenever they choose, prior to final discharge of the principal, and prior to termination of the effectiveness of the bond by forfeiture or otherwise. There is authority for the proposition that the principal may be taken by the bail at night or on Sunday, but arrests should not be made at night or on Sunday except in case of pressing necessity."

Section 122. Place of arrest; pursuit
(This section states that "bail is not dependent on process" and the defendant may be "pursued into a sister state and detained.")

Section 123. Effect of forcible entry
"Since arrest of a criminal defendant by his bail is regarded as in the nature of arrest and detention of a criminal rather than as service of process, sureties on a bail bond are entitled to break open the doors of the home of the principal to effect his arrest where the principal refuses to surrender himself on notice to do so. However, where the sureties on a bail bond or recognizance commit acts not authorized by law, for the purpose of arresting the principal, they may be subjected to liability for the actual damages they cause thereby."

West Virginia
From: Criminal Procedure; Bail
62-1C-14. Bailpiece; issuance to surety; taking accused into custody
"A bailpiece is a certificate stating that the bail became such for the accused in a particular case and the amount thereof. Upon demand therefor, the court, justice or clerk shall issue to the surety a bailpiece. Any officer having authority to execute a warrant of arrest shall assist the surety holding such bailpiece to take the accused into custody and produce him before the court or justice. The surety may take the accused into custody and surrender him to the court or justice without such bailpiece."

Wisconsin

From: Criminal Procedure

969.14 Surrender of principal by surety

"(1) When the sureties desire to be discharged from the obligations of their bond, they may arrest the principal and deliver him to the sheriff of the county in which the action against him is pending.

(2) The sureties shall, at the time of surrendering the principal, deliver to the sheriff a certified copy of the original warrant and of the order admitting him to bail and of the bond thereon; such delivery of these documents shall be sufficient authority for the sheriff to receive and retain the principal until he is otherwise bailed or discharged.

(3) Upon the delivery of the principal as provided herein, the sureties may apply to the court for an order discharging them from liability as sureties; and upon satisfactory proof being made that this section has been complied with the court shall make an order discharging them from liability."

Wyoming

1-298. Authority of bail to arrest defendant or have him arrested

"The bail may, for the purpose of surrendering the defendant, arrest him at any time or place before he is finally charged, or, by a written authority endorsed on a certified copy of the undertaking may empower any person of suitable age and discretion to do so."

11. Glossary

BOUNTY HUNTING OR BAIL ARREST IS essentially a legal affair complete with all the legalese this profession is capable of producing.

The words below represent some of the more commonly used terms found in the bail bond business, the courts, and law enforcement. These are from *Black's Law Dictionary* which can be found in any library.

Bail: The surety or sureties who procure the release of a person under arrest, by becoming responsible for his appearance at the time and place designated. Those persons who become sureties for the appearance of the defendant in court.

Bail Bond: A written undertaking, executed by the defendant or one or more sureties, that the defendant designated in such instrument will, while at liberty as a result of an order fixing bail and of the execution of a bail bond in satisfaction thereof, appear in a designated criminal action or proceeding when his attendance is required and otherwise render himself amenable to the orders and processes of the court, and that in the event he fails to do so, the signers of the bond will pay to the court the amount of money specified in the order fixing bail.

Bail Point Scale: System whereby a predetermined number of points are given for all positive aspects of the defendant's background. The total number of points determine whether the defendant will be released on his own recognizance or the amount of bail to be set for his release.

Bailable: Capable of being bailed; admitting of bail; authorizing or requiring bail.

Bailable Action: One in which the defendant is entitled to be discharged from arrest only upon giving bond to answer.

Bailable Offense: One for which the prisoner may be admitted to bail.

Bounty: A gratuity, or an unusual or additional benefit conferred upon, or compensation paid to, a class of persons. . . . *Reward* is more proper in the case of a single service, which can be only once performed, and therefore will be earned only by the person or co-operative persons who succeed while others fail, e.g., capture of a fugitive.

Cash Bail Bond: A sum of money, in the amount designated in an order fixing bail, posted by a defendant or by another person on his behalf with a court or other authorized public officer upon condition that such money will be forfeited if the defendant does not comply with the directions of a court requiring his attendance at the criminal action or proceeding involved and does not otherwise render himself amenable to the orders and processes of the court.

Exoneration of Bail: The release from liability of the sureties on a bail bond either by their surrender of their principal to the proper authorities or by his surrender of himself before the day stipulated in the bond. (6 Am Jur 91,105).

Surety: One who undertakes to pay money or to do any other act in event that his principal fails therein. One bound with his principal for the payment of a sum of money or for the performance of some duty or promise and who is entitled to be indemnified by some one who ought to have paid or performed if payment or performance be enforced against him. Everyone who incurs a liability in person or estate for the benefit of another, without sharing in the consideration, stands in the position of a "surety," whatever may be the form of his obligation.